# The #Pray4 Principle

# The #Pray4 Principle

## Why prayer is still important in a secular age

*Alexander Lee*

DARTON·LONGMAN + TODD

First published in 2013 by
Darton, Longman and Todd Ltd
1 Spencer Court
140 – 142 Wandsworth High Street
London SW18 4JJ

ISBN: 978-0-232-52982-1

Bible quotes are from the New International Version Bible (NIV)
unless otherwise stated.

Phototypeset by Kerrypress Ltd, Luton, Bedfordshire.
Printed and bound by Bell & Bain, Glasgow.

# Contents

# Foreword

For a week in March 2012 the world of football united in rallying around stricken Fabrice Muamba, praying that the Bolton midfielder would win his greatest battle.

From top managers such as Arsène Wenger to the youngest fans at the lowliest grounds around the country, we were all encouraged to pray for the critically ill England Under-21 star.

It really was an unprecedented outpouring of love, hope and prayers from all across the world for Muamba, as he fought for his life at the London Chest Hospital in Bethnal Green.

In the days following Fabrice's collapse, football fans flocked to Bolton's stadium to remember their hero. They stood in silence, heads bowed in prayer as they laid cards, flowers, scarves and shirts emblazoned with get-well messages outside the gates of the Reebok ground.

These were not just Bolton fans either. Many were fans of different teams coming together in support of the popular midfielder and it certainly put things into perspective as petty footballing rivalries were forgotten and fans considered what really mattered.

On the pitch, former teammate Gary Cahill lifted his shirt to reveal the message: 'Pray for Muamba' after scoring for Chelsea against Leicester in the FA Cup quarter finals. Other footballing superstars followed suit in games all across the planet. The hashtag #PrayForMuamba was being used on Twitter as fans and players sent their own messages of support. It was a week of unprecedented and sustained prayer for the young star.

And, as we know, those prayers were answered. A medical miracle unfolded before our eyes. This book unpacks the inside story behind that week's events in a way that will excite and motivate you to believe anew in a God who hears and still answers prayer today, and is very much in the habit of doing the miraculous.

# 1.

# The Pray4Muamba Campaign

An away goal at White Hart Lane is nothing to be sniffed at. Since Harry Redknapp rescued Spurs from the relegation zone back in October 2008, the men in white have become a force to be reckoned with in the English Premier League.

Two years after Harry's appointment, the world became aware of Tottenham Hotspur's potential when the London team claimed the scalp of Inter Milan and overcame a resolute A.C. Milan in the Champions League. Being a Welshman, I often keep an eye on Tottenham's results and credit the Cardiff born midfielder Gareth Bale for their resurgence. (This doesn't always go down well in North London.)

An FA Cup match on 17 March 2012, however, saw a struggling Lancashire team take the lead at the White Hart Lane Cauldron. Fiery Scotsman Owen Coyle had instilled a fighting spirit among his Bolton Wanderers side who went ahead early in the game with a deflected Darren Pratley header.

Spurs soon dampened the away fans' celebrations with a quick equaliser when Bale supplied Kyle Walker, who subsequently headed home. Bolton needed a cup win to boost morale amid a relegation battle in the league. Spurs needed a victory to galvanise their squad-challenging for another Champions League spot.

Forty minutes were on the clock and the game statistics were as follows:

*Shots*
Spurs: 6    Bolton: 5

*Shots on target*
Spurs: 4    Bolton: 0

*Corners*
Spurs: 3    Bolton: 3

*Fouls*
Spurs: 2    Bolton: 0

*Score*
Spurs: 1    Bolton: 1

As the Wanderers' keeper prepared to punt the ball upfield, the packed White Hart Lane crowd grew quiet. An event that silenced a stadium went on to stun world football and beyond. The young Bolton midfielder Fabrice Muamba collapsed between the halfway line and the penalty box.

The 23-year-old Anglo-African footballer was lying face down on the North London soil with no pulse, no breath and no response. Within seconds the medics attended the scene and began trying to resuscitate Muamba. Amongst the medical team were Bolton Wanderers' team doctor Jonathan Tobin and cardiologist Dr Andrew Deaner, who happened to be sitting in the stands as a Spurs fan.

Muamba had suffered a cardiac arrest and, according to Dr Tobin, registered no muscular heartbeat for nearly 80 minutes. In effect, Fabrice Muamba had died in front of more than 30,000 people.

Attempts to kick-start Muamba's heart were ongoing until he was taken to the London Chest Hospital, where a further 30 minutes of resuscitation took place.

Speaking to national press, Dr Tobin stated that the heart eventually registered a beat after 'much fist hammering and 15 electric shocks'.

For years, medical experts have stipulated that a human brain starved of oxygen for more than four minutes faces a serious risk of fatality or severe long-term damage. Muamba's brain was without a healthy supply of oxygen for 78 minutes.

News broadcasters across the world were replaying the traumatic pictures while Muamba lay in an induced coma. The news coming from the hospital was cold and clear: the heart was beating but the damage to the brain was unknown at this moment.

Understandably the match was called off, as the sporting world stood, quietly waiting, faced with the very real risk of losing a much-loved talent. From the brief reports coming from the hospital media team and the sombre tones of Bolton Manager Owen Coyle the future looked bleak.

Amid the media frenzy and out of the ashes of such a bleak predicament, the quiet voices of Muamba's family uttered a phrase that would go on to unite millions. His fiancée, Shauna Magunda, and parents Marcel and Gertrude, didn't ask for sympathy but instead encouraged the watching world to simply 'Pray for Muamba'. It was a request that millions and millions of people would agree to.

The days and weeks that followed Muamba's heart failure saw a prayer campaign that dwarfed any recent evangelical attempts to inspire a spiritual awakening. Social networks became engulfed with the Pray4Muamba theme while national press published front-page headlines including, 'God is in control' (*The Sun*) and 'In God's hands' (*The Daily Star*). Premier League A-List celebrities fashioned T-shirts underneath their jerseys that read 'Pray4Muamba' in bold letters. Sportsmen from different fields, countries and continents wore similar T-shirts urging viewers and fans to also 'Pray4Muamba'. Some of the greatest overseas players ever to grace the game of football travelled to support the unassuming midfielder, whose future remained uncertain, and potentially very short.

## UNITY IN INJURY

Both sets of supporters chanted Muamba's name as he was taken off the pitch on a stretcher during the infamous game. The united cheering marked the start of a global stance that lasted until the seemingly impossible became reality. Or to quote Dr Andrew Deaner: 'If you're going to use the term "miraculous" it could be used here.'

Almost unbelievably, the Muamba family was reporting that Fabrice was moving his arms and legs, responding to questions and recognising family members at the London Chest Hospital, just days after the incident. The news shocked experienced medics and lifted an entire nation.

As a journalist I instantly began speaking with friends in the medical world to find out the truth surrounding such a condition. I am familiar with emotional situations getting the better of common sense and wanted to be sure that this was genuinely a medical anomaly. I found that many of those who work in medicine were genuinely shocked that anyone could have survived such an ordeal so well and so quickly.

Dr Deaner, who had been so important to the immediate recovery process, went on to report how Fabrice was able to make a joke just two days after his cardiac arrest. As the young man was taken out of a medically induced coma, the doctor said: 'I understand you're a very good footballer'. Fabrice cheekily responded with: 'I try.'

5

Within the sceptical side of my mind I expected the good news of Muamba's initial recovery to bring the Pray4Muamba campaign to an end but, on the contrary, it acted as a catalyst for celebration and increased support.

During the first week of April, Fabrice turned 24-years-old in hospital and was walking the corridors of the ward with his renowned smile encouraging those around him. Less than a month after collapsing live on television, Muamba was discharged from hospital.

I watched the public support grow like flames in a dry forest and was astonished at how passionate a secular society welcomed the idea of prayer. In a country where theism seems to have taken a battering from Richard Dawkins and thousands of similar voices singing from the same faithless hymn book, how did the word 'pray' become so popular?

During my training as a reporter, I developed a sceptic's eye. But as I watched some of my journalist colleagues, perhaps far more cynical than I, Tweet and blog about how important it was to 'Pray 4 Muamba', I knew I had to rethink my stance on faith in twenty-first century Great Britain.

If I am being honest, I had developed a belief that God had been kicked out of the secular conversation in the British Isles. But watching how quickly people turned to the notion of 'prayer' when a young man's heart had failed, when a young man's life was in grave danger, made me consider the philosophical musings by the writer of Ecclesiastes:

> He has made everything beautiful in its time. He has also set eternity in the human heart; yet no one can fathom what God has done from beginning to end.
>
> (3:11)

And that is what it felt like in the UK. It felt like I had discovered in the deepest corner of the UK human collective, a corporate desire to pray when control was no longer in the hands of men and women. In pubs, coffee shops and churches across the country, people were reading about Fabrice's recovery progress as if he was someone they knew personally. There was genuine hope, fear and faith being expressed from the lips of non-churchgoing adults And as they expressed their concerns through millions of social media messages to Fabrice, his family and Bolton Wanderers FC, each message was collated under the umbrella 'Pray4Muamba'.

I often wondered what the avid atheist or the timid Christian thought when seeing a barrage of this repeated phrase. After all, it would have been more politically correct to say, 'Pause 4 Muamba' or indeed 'Remember Muamba' but it was not to be. An Anglican church leader in York commented that he had never seen the word 'pray' scattered throughout the community in his entire ministry.

The obvious questions for a practicing Evangelical Christian included, 'To whom are these masses praying?' and 'Do they even know how to pray?' And the truth is that a lot of prayers muttered by the un-churched are usually done so in silence. From my work as an evangelist with York's Saint Michael Le Belfrey Church back in 2005, I learnt that the prayers of a reluctant believer are often directed thoughts, aimed at a being more powerful than the individual; someone or something to be revered in times of crisis. What I also discovered in the streets and pubs of York was that 'prayer' among the un-churched could often be seen as 'meditation' by an evangelical. It's more of an instinctive submission than a crafted intercession. Both valid expressions of faith in a higher being, but the former is often muttered when all seems lost.

## THE LAST RESORT?

The spiritual aftermath of the Muamba injury and recovery led me to a fascinating exploration. I wanted to find out why so many of us humans feel the need to lift the eyes of our soul as a last resort. I quickly found that it is not just a contemporary reaction to hardship by any means, but a habit formed by men and women over thousands of years.

As I researched historical accounts of spiritual reactions to physical problems, it was not hard to see that human suffering was almost always the common denominator. Whether it is physical or emotional pain, something of the nature of hardship seems to move the human spirit into a unique action. When our control of a situation dwindles, and the situation seemingly dwarfs our own power, something beyond our physical DNA humbles itself. And as twenty-first century Western beings so used to routine and comfort, we certainly face an unknown beast when looking at suffering.

What is for certain is that a painful situation like watching a finely tuned athlete collapse on a football pitch slows our perspective down. I remember the shared feeling of subdued shock when I watched the Spurs – Bolton game, sipping a drink in my local pub beside 30 local patrons. Each guest slowed down in both speech and movement. We knew we were all encountering something that was beyond surface-level life. This was an example of humanity facing an unknown entity. For the trained medical eye as well as the average guy, death seemed a very real outcome.

And for all the answers modern medicine has offered our country, existence beyond the grave is still a taboo subject. The attitude I have seen among British men particularly is one that seldom discusses death. 'You only live once,' and 'I'll sleep when I'm dead,' are typical phrases thrown around when the idea of death sneaks into a conversation.

As the Christian message becomes more and more alien to the upcoming un-churched generation, life after death has almost been placed on a blank canvas. Nobody dare offer a heaven versus hell answer, yet the idea of this life being totally meaningless still does not seem to sit right with many people. And because so many people still cling to a subconscious hope that there is external meaning and direction in life, watching Muamba's heart failure on live TV evoked three familiar questions:

1) What is happening?
2) Why is this happening?
3) Is there any hope?

From my discussions with friends and strangers with regard to the Muamba incident, and similar public tragedies, I would argue that the aforementioned questions actually come naturally to the average crowd of people. They are not questions we have been taught to ask when watching events of suffering, but have somehow been buried in our human nature. I would also argue that when our perspective is slowed down by a specific ordeal, the gears of our deepest beings begin to shift. Though the intensity of Muamba's condition was increasing by the minute, the state of mind of the nation was seemingly being placed on pause. I believe that it is in these hours and days when we are in a state of pause that something spiritual happens.

Author and specialist in contemporary spiritual thought Brian Draper picks up on the notion of slowing down for the soul to initiate in his book *Spiritual Intelligence*:

> As we try to slow down and shut out the background noise of a culture stuck on fast forward, as we practice contemplation, dwell

within silence, and switch off the ever-working ego-driven mind, we offer ourselves the chance to remember not just who we were to be, as individuals, but who we were created to be as humanity.

If the writer of Ecclesiastes is right when he says that the things of God are written into the human heart, it should be no surprise then, that when we are faced with the threat of losing our human experience, prayer becomes our last resort. Draper's argument that we 'remember who we were created to be' begins to make more sense when we look back on the unity inspired by both tragedy and prayer.

Of course, prayer is not the only last resort in moments of crisis. Many people offered their condolences to the Muamba household by stating they were 'thinking of Fabrice'. Indeed many others reported they were sending 'positive thoughts' as well as 'crossing their fingers'.

But one would have to admit that the alternative approaches to inputting into Muamba's recovery were all examples of humans acting in their own strength. The difference between thinking positively and prayer is that the latter requires a sense of submission, while the former places trust directly into the human condition.

In the sixth chapter of John's account in the New Testament, the core disciples were faced with an incredibly difficult decision. After Jesus spoke to 5000 followers, he underlined the true cost of what it meant to be a 'Christian' amid Roman and Jewish opposition. On hearing about the hardship that was to come, everyone abandoned Jesus except the twelve.

It was a moment of incredible pressure and stress for the dozen disciples. Their options were to either return to their former lives in their own strength, or submit to Christ and his will. The text shows how Jesus himself went on to ask the twelve if they also wanted to return to their former lives and abandon the mission. Simon Peter spoke on behalf of the twelve and underlined the driving force behind this notion of 'the last resort'. After the mass exodus, in the stillness of the moment, Simon Peter replied: 'Lord, to whom shall we go? You have the words of eternal life.' (John 6:68)

The truth is Simon and the twelve did have some-where else to go. There were other last resorts to turn to. Like the majority of people in this instance, they could have returned to their old homes and jobs. However, each of these alternatives felt like no-goers compared to turning to face Jesus. They knew that something 'eternal' was in front of them.

The disciples modelled another way of dealing with difficulty. They could have quite easily responded with a twee response justifying why they were not comfortable submitting their trust to an external source. But like Fabrice Muamba's family, they dared to trust something or someone beyond their personal opinions, philosophies and theolo-gies. They dared to have a basic faith in the face of destruction.

Nicky Chiswell picked up on this notion of the last resort in her popular song 'Where else have we to go?' where she writes:

> Come all you who labour, you who are weighed down, you who thirst and hunger for the right.
> There is truth and meaning, Mercy, rest and hope.
> True salvation comes through Jesus Christ.
> Where else have we to go, when you alone have words of eternal life?
>
> © 1998 Nicky Chiswell

But as we see in both Muamba's injury and recovery, the 'meaning' that the song explores, doesn't always come immediately, or with instant clarity. How can we prove that prayer has more of an effect than positive thought and the crossing of fingers? We will explore this idea in more detail during further chapters.

As well as looking at historical accounts of people groups turning to prayer in crisis moments we will also be looking at the question: Why prayer? Despite our advances in science and technology, our dwindling traditional UK church attendance, and the fervent wave of popular atheism, why is prayer still an inclusive notion? Prayer continues to play a huge part in lives of those inside and outside the 'church' posing many questions for the Western Christianity.

If indeed prayer is the last resort, could it be one of the few expressions of faith that overrides a person's academic understanding of the human experience? Is prayer a realistic tool for awakening our spiritual journey and is it a viable starting point for those looking to discover something deeper than material-istic gain?

Whatever our feelings towards prayer, and whether or not we think it is something that can be adopted by those who wouldn't call themselves 'Christians', it is a subject that is worth contemplat-ing.

From the live Twitter feeds written at the time of Muamba's injury, which will bring this chapter to a close below, we see that people from all sorts of backgrounds felt totally comfortable at the idea of praying for a wounded man. This circumstance alone should entice us to rethink how, why and where we feel prayer should be encouraged and experienced.

Later on we will also get Muamba's thoughts on the prayer movement based around his wellbeing and how he feels prayer should fit in today's post-religious society.

### Twitter feeds

Just left the hospital. Love you so much man! Keep fighting. Everybody please pray for him he's an amazing man and friend.
Johan Djourou, Arsenal defender and former col-league of Fabrice Muamba. (@JohanDjourou)

Terrible what happened with Muamba during the game. We're all praying for him.

Rafael van der Vaart, Spurs' midfielder; was one of the players on the pitch during the incident. (@rafvdaart)

> I seriously hope my best friend in football is OK. Stay strong bro, please please stay strong. God is with you remember that.

Justin Hoyte, Middlesbrough defender who played alongside Fabrice Muamba in the Arsenal youth team. (@justinhoyte84)

## Mail Online Forum

> I'm not religious, but thank god!

Mama Twinkletoes, London, 20/3/2012 19:25

> May the powers that be continue to watch over him and give him the strength to make a full recovery.

Vivien, West Midlands, 20/3/2012 18:08

> I sincerely hope Fabrice makes a full recovery and is able to return home very soon to his lovely family. Very best wishes to Fabrice and we will keep praying for you!

Maggie, Shropshire, 20/3/2012 16:50

# 2.

# The last resort?
# Second nature

> *We do not have to present our prayers to God in order to disclose to him our needs and desires, but in order to make ourselves realise that we need to have recourse to his help in these matters.*
>
> Thomas Aquinas

One of the points well covered on the introductory course to Christianity 'Alpha' is that, if there is a God, wouldn't he want to communicate with his creation. The popular Alpha course goes on to explain that effective communication is always two-way, and not just a monologue. Throughout the Bible we see how God speaks to people from a variety of different backgrounds, regardless of their upbringing. We also see him speak through a variety of different means. Some incidents show him using conventional conversation, other times he chooses some incredibly unorthodox methods. Whatever our individual doctrinal thoughts on specific Bible stories are, we cannot disagree with the fact that the

God painted in both the Old and New Testaments is a God who loves to communicate. It would make sense then, that if we are created by a communicative being, we are expected to communicate back. In theory this reads quite well. However, as we take greater corporate leaps into secularism, it is not the theory of theism that is becoming more and more estranged, but the practice of theism. After all, people are very keen to discuss and debate theism in a variety of forums, but actually practicing prayer is a different matter entirely.

*Guardian* writer Andrew Brown was one of the first journalists to explore the prayer awakening during the Muamba incident. Just days after the cardiac arrest, Brown wrote: 'This isn't marginalised religion. In fact it is such a public demonstration of faith and prayer that it's hard to reconcile it with our normal worldview.' In his observations of the spiritual reaction to such a brutal physical event, Brown commented on how the notion of religion was indeed something boxed off by the average British resident; however, the notion of prayer still resonated with lots of people. If this is true, we must not *just* ask ourselves if prayer is a last resort for many people, but also if it can become second nature to a created soul.

In Mark Vernon's recent publication *The Big Questions: God*, the philosophy writer picks up on the comparison between daily life and prayer. He argues: 'Prayer is likened to breathing. You can skip more prayers than you can breaths, and hold off from praying much longer than you can hold off from breathing, but the analogy implies that prayer is an activity that sustains the soul, much as breath sustains biological life. It may be performed absent-mindedly. It may be troubled or laboured. Few breaths are as satisfying as a lungful of Alpine air; so too prayers.'

But what does it mean to pray absent-mindedly? One has to admit that the way prayer is often demonstrated in many local UK churches is that of an ordered expression vocalised to cover specific subjects. Prayer usually starts and stops at clear points. Congregational onlookers can clearly see where prayer fits within a church service. There is nothing absent minded or spontaneous with the prayer slots in many local church services. But this 'traditional' expression of prayer is not what was behind the Pray4Muamba movement. The traditional styles of prayer, much like many other evangelical aspects of Christendom, do not come as second nature to the average Brit.

This poses a challenging question for us as twenty-first-century Christians. Is there a form of prayerful communication between the created and the creator that comes as second nature? In Paul's first letter to the Thessalonians he gave passionate and perplexing advice: 'Rejoice always, *pray continually*, give thanks in all circumstances; for this is God's will for you in Christ Jesus.' (1 Thessalonians 5:16–18)

Did the Apostle seriously mean we should be praying to God with spoken words continuously? Of

course not. For how could we sustain any friend-
ships with our fellow humans if we were constantly
verbalising our thoughts to an invisible deity. Paul
delves deeper into this notion in the book of
Romans: 'In the same way, the Spirit helps us in our
weakness. We do not know what we ought to pray
for, but the Spirit himself intercedes for us through
wordless groans. And he who searches our hearts
knows the mind of the Spirit, because the Spirit
intercedes for God's people in accordance with the
will of God. And we know that in all things God
works for the good of those who love him, who have
been called according to his purpose.' (Romans
8:26–28)

As someone who was not brought up with any
knowledge of the Christian story, I too can share
Paul's opinion on prayer. During the days following
my 'conversion experience' I was fully aware that
my prayer vocabulary was barely existent. However,
looking back on that time eleven years on, I can say
it was a period where I prayed more than I ever have
since. Though it was not my tongue, or indeed my
brain, that was leading the dialogue between my
creator and me, but more my soul. It was something
deep within my being voicing its thankfulness, its
concerns, its questions and its desires. I can testify
that as soon I had put my atom of faith into a
communicative God, prayer was indeed second
nature. But it was not the sort of praying I had
envisaged before my conversion. One of the new
aspects of my personality that changed my worldly

perspective was that I was consciously directing my thought process to God. Mundane thoughts, day-dreams, anxious moments, everything was pushed to an invisible being who I had welcomed into my life.

However, the lines of pure doctrine begin to blur when I realise that, though I can point to a specific time when I found faith, I can also remember times I had prayed prior to that moment. What happened to those prayers; the prayers of the seemingly faith-less? Are they heard at all? Again, Vernon addresses this issue wonderfully in *The Big Questions: God*: 'First, it can't be the case that only believers can pray. It might be assumed that this is so, on the grounds that only the believer knows who they are praying to. But I think this actually gets prayer the wrong way around. The most heartfelt prayers are often spontaneous. They are cries of help or shouts of thanks. Whether or not anyone is there to hear them is immaterial. In fact, if you were absolutely con-vinced there was someone listening to you, you might not cry or shout at all. You might reason that your divine hearer knows what you need or feel before you do yourself. This is to say that prayer has directionality. It originates in the minds and mouths of men. It can be done by agnostics.'

It is fair to say that none of us can be sure that God will grant us our prayer requests just because we have faith. Even the most faithful of believers have prayed for things that never came to pass. So if the answers to our prayers do not always reflect the amount of passion we have in our faith, what then is the criteria for prayers that are answered and prayers that are rejected?

Many conservative evangelicals may argue that true prayer can only come after true repentance. But nobody would disagree with the notion that only God sees the heart; the place where the Bible says repentance begins. So if God alone can see the human heart, then shouldn't we be more hesitant to predict who can and cannot pray? The seeds of prayer planted in my soul, years before my conversion were very influential in my journey. Though on the surface of my life I was antagonistic to Christian theology, the cogs of my heart were slowly changing. Prayers were being born and, albeit slowly and unconventionally, my soul was coming alive.

Eye witnesses to Jesus' death heard a thief beside the saviour mumble a desperate plea for salvation. I would argue that not many religious types would have put their neck out and called that very thief a 'man of faith' or a 'godly' man. But Jesus went on to display his sovereignty on the cross by deciding the future of the thief. One of the temptations for an Evangelical Christian is to begin to believe he or she owns the monopoly of true doctrine. We can testify how God has moved in our own personal stories and find it very difficult to engage with stories that are vastly different. For instance, a conservative may struggle to hear someone claim to have seen or heard from God in a dream. A charismatic may struggle to hear someone state that they only hear from God through words on the pages of the Bible. But whatever side of the doctrinal fence we sit on, we must be careful that we don't become biased schoolyard football captains deciding who can and can't play for their team. If prayer is one of the few traits of the Christian faith not to be rejected in current secularism, how should we equip non-churchgoers with helpful resources and information on prayer? How do we plant seeds of prayer in the lives of others?

Reflecting on the Pray4 Principle of prayer amid a secular society, we need to ask if prayer actually comes as second nature to the average man or woman. I'd suggest that publicly spoken prayer does not come naturally, at least. Working as an evangelist for Saint Michael Le Belfrey Church in York, I rarely found a new believer or indeed an agnostic who was comfortable with praying out loud in front of others. To be honest, I struggled to find many Christians who were comfortable in doing this. And one must be honest that during the Pray4Muamba movement, I cannot recall any non-churched individuals leading public prayers for the footballer. But I would not argue that this disqualifies the notion that people were praying at all. Some may say that the lack of public showmanship surrounding the outpouring of prayer qualifies the event further.

We see Jesus ripping up the rule book of prayer in Matthew's account. Challenging the conventional way of praying among the religious leaders, he said: 'But when you pray, go into your room, close the door and pray to your Father, who is unseen. Then your Father, who sees what is done in secret, will reward you.' (Matthew 6:6)

So if Jesus is stating that prayer is something beyond crafted words of intercessions spoken beautifully from a lectern or pulpit, and is something we are encouraged to perform in the solitude of our own lives by the very author of life, then maybe the idea of prayer becoming second nature to the human soul is not that hard to believe. Why would the Son of God encourage a crowd of average Joes to develop a prayer life if the human soul could not get to grips with prayer itself?

## INSTINCT

Millwall FC chaplain Reverend Owen Beamont has experience with the dynamic link between prayer and those involved with sport. During an interview with *Guardian* writer Andrew Brown he spoke honestly about how footballers process the idea of prayer. He said: 'They pray from instinct, like the rest of us, unless we think we know better.'

On first reading Revd Beamont's remarks on how we may be tempted to think we 'know better' on the topic of prayer, I found myself incredibly challenged. As someone who has taught the Bible, led prayer groups and written Bible studies for national Christian charities, I have to confess that I am tempted to take the spiritual high ground when it comes to some aspects of the Christian faith. But the more I study the Scriptures and seek mentorship

23

from those older in the faith, the more I see that God is a living being who is desperately trying to become a pragmatic part of my daily routine. Now, as I strive to become a man who 'prays continually', I know I have to battle with the temptation to box my prayer life into the quiet section of a Sunday church service. Surely if God is a communicative God, and Paul's inspired writing in Thessalonians tells us to pray continually, then my human instinct has a massive part to play in my spiritual growth. There needs to be a juxtaposition of my soul's groans to God and my gut reaction to life's unpredictable hurdles. But how do we envelop our random lives with prayer, while at the same time living our lives to the full?

Perhaps Vernon's reflections on prayer can shed some light on its complexities: 'Prayer is more like seeing the point of a work of art. You may not understand it at first glance. It may also be ruined by being hung in the wrong place, or with you in front of it with the wrong frame of mind. Only gradually, with patience, care and discipline does the point of it emerge.' (*The Big Questions: God*)

I would argue that after reading the prayerful reactions of the non-religious football fans, instinctive prayer is of important value the human soul. Maybe that is what it means to 'pray continually'; an individual who chooses to make his or her port of call something higher.

However, the soul cannot grow to its full potential on aimless prayers of reaction. Without the individual looking to discover what Vernon calls 'the point' of prayer, then the prayer itself could become a selfish act. Prayer has to be a starting point to something more. I do not think it is a case of prayer being *either* instinctive or crafted verbally, but a case of both. We must grapple with the idea of prayer being a lucid expression of faith voiced with words, groans, thoughts, writings, texts, or indeed online campaigns titled Pray4Muamba. Prayer is not one of the above, but potentially all of the above.

It is hard not to be protective over the core aspects of evangelical Christianity. Prayer is one of the most sacred parts that make up our faith, and something that we do not always like to see being taken lightly. We see within the beautiful and painful atonement on the cross that Jesus' death itself became a game-changer for prayer. We know that through accepting the sacrifice of Christ we are given the opportunity to approach God not just as a creator, but now as a father. Due to events surrounding this post-cross grace, many Christians are uncomfortable with those appearing over-familiar with prayer to the Father, God. Indeed, in Paul's letter to the Romans, he says: 'The Spirit you received does not make you slaves, so that you live in fear again; rather, the Spirit you received brought about your adoption to sonship. And by him we cry "Abba", Father.' (Romans 8:15)

Paul is talking about a sacred adoption on a cosmic scale, crossing cities, countries and even generations. And because of the scale of sacrifice needed for this spiritual shift, prayer is not something we should be crass about. One has to sympathise with the believers who struggled to process the Pray4Muamba appeal. There is, however, a thin line between *respecting* a sacred ritual, and religiously *claiming* the ritual as your own. Does prayer belong in church and church only? No, for we see Jesus telling the people to take prayer home with them. Is there a part of the human instinct that is inclined to pray in times of crisis? Yes, the Muamba incident shows us how quickly the word 'prayer' became an international buzz word. Can prayer become like second nature for the average person? I believe that might well be God's plan for his creation.

The Bible shows us that developing a prayer life that goes beyond Twitter campaigns takes effort on our part, but more importantly, the work of God's Spirit. A Christian faith that is heading towards maturity must evolve in the area of discernment. And as Christians growing in the faith, we must look to discern between positive spiritual growth and mere phases of commercial expression. Writing honestly, I am aware that as a journalist there's a trained cynic's eye that sits in the core of my being. I have seen similar traits in many of my friends who have trained as business professionals. Something draws us to scepticism. The examples of Jesus' ministry however, encourage us to see the fickle line between cynicism and discernment. One may argue that the Muamba incident was a case of cultural fashion, nothing more than an alternative wristband or a hairstyle. Others may see the positive continued appeal of prayer within circles of secularism. As an adopted son of the Christian faith, I have been challenged to choose optimism.

As we contemplate the idea that prayer may still be a second nature attribute for many people, we must not become naïve and presume a reactionary prayer campaign changes the spiritual make up of the UK. It may be a prime example of how quickly public opinion can seemingly shift from a place of faithlessness to a point of prayer, but Biblically, we need to be ready to see mustard seeds of faith mature. As it says in Paul's letter to the Church in Ephesus: 'And I pray that you, being rooted and established in love, may have power, together with all the Lord's holy people, to grasp how wide and long and high and deep is the love of Christ, and to know this love that surpasses knowledge – that you may be filled to the measure of all the fullness of God.' (Ephesians 3:17–19)

Fullness is the right word towards the end of that passage. Praying for one situation is righteous, but it should not fulfil our spiritual thirst. God has count-less adventures set before us to reveal God's fulfil-ment. Adventures that will take up the entirety of our lives.

# 3.

# Echoes

Each sailor had their own religion. During the calm of the night they would each wax lyrical about their unique interpretation of what they believed. Some of them explained the names of gods they worshipped; others amalgamated theologies and thought to create a faith collage. They were floating blends of belief sailing across a blue foreign canvas. These sailors were happy to have their own perspective on how the world came to be, how it began to spin and how it would eventually end.

Part of their duty as mariners was to transport travellers from Joppa to Tarshish. There was one traveller who would test the very fabric of their religions; his name was Jonah. For as soon as he stepped onboard, a storm began to brew on the horizon. It was as if this particular passenger had nature's target on his back.

The storm smashed into the boat relentlessly while Jonah slept below deck. An order had already been passed for each sailor to call on the name of whatever god he believed in, in the hope that something in the heavens would protect their boat, which was literally being torn to bits.

It didn't take long for them to work out that, somehow, Jonah was linked to this storm. Despite them calling on their own gods, they decided to confront the forlorn stranger for answers: 'What do you believe, and what have you done?'

In that moment, on a rough journey to Tarshish, Jonah knew his life had caught up with him. However hard he ran, however far he sailed, the consequences of his decision prior to boarding would never leave him: 'I worship the Lord, the God of heaven, who made the sea and the dry land. He asked something of me, but I ran away. I am still running. If you want to live, you need to throw me overboard.'

The sailors were faced with an incredibly difficult decision. They knew in the depths of their souls that Jonah was telling the truth. They also knew they were doomed if he stayed onboard. So, taking the Hebrew's advice, they threw Jonah to the megalith waves. But as the ancient story reveals, that's not all they did. Interestingly, this group of diverse thinkers, none of whom identified themselves as a Hebrew, instantly began to pray. They did not pray to a distant 'god', nor did they call on the deities of folklore, they prayed to the one who is called 'Lord'. As the Book of Jonah states:

> Instead, the men did their best to row back to land. But they could not, for the sea grew even

wilder than before. Then they cried out to the Lord, 'Please, Lord, do not let us die for taking this man's life. Do not hold us accountable for killing an innocent man, for you, Lord, have done as you pleased.' Then they took Jonah and threw him overboard and the raging sea grew calm. At this the men greatly feared the Lord, and they offered a sacrifice to the Lord and made vows to him.'

Jonah 1:13–16

There are lessons to be learnt about the situation surrounding the prayer of the mariners. Specific aspects of the psychology within this passage are still played out in arenas to this day. One of the more striking features in this section of Old Testament Scripture is the human potential for spiritual *adaptation*.

## ADAPT TO SURVIVE

It does not take a genius to see how quick the sailors were to adapt their religious stance in an attempt to save their lives. Though the willingness to adapt such an integral part of the human stance is intriguing, what is even more fascinating is that each sailor already had the ability to do such a thing without having to leave the ship. Each of them spoke personally and vulnerably to 'The Lord' despite having seemingly no prior experience of such an act.

If I, as a Christian in the UK, were asked to lead a Buddhist meditative session, I would have no idea where to start. If I were challenged to deliver a Sikh reflection or a Hindu ritual, I would be totally clueless from beginning to end. But adapting typical vocabulary, into a prayer directed to an all-encompassing sovereign Lord was doable for a group of terrified sailors. In fact, this desperate group of working-class mariners, exhausted in the middle of an onslaught, completed this prayer-task with ease. They prayed honestly, with no priest or pastor, no choir or temple, to the Lord. A question must be voiced then; why can humans adapt such a colossal spiritual stance in such a short amount of time? Can it be possible that each created man and woman already has the tools needed to become a person of prayer?

Like the mariners, we too live in a culture where spirituality is as varied and colourful as an English autumn. However, we also exist on an island where prayer is not totally alien to the average person. Whether it is memories of saying the Lord's Prayer in school, witnessing a traditional church wedding or indeed hearing prayers at a funeral, the notion itself is not radically new.

Paul Y. Cho, pastor of one the largest Evangelical churches on the planet, credits the growth of his Korean congregation largely to prayer. In his book *Prayer: Key to Revival* he says: 'Our problem has been that we have thought about prayer, read about prayer and even received teaching regarding prayer, but we just have not prayed ... Our potential is much greater than any of us have ever realised.'

It is this prayer *potential* Cho speaks of that we see so wonderfully in the Book of Jonah. Of course the story goes on to reveal that even the main character needed to face his own prayer potential while buried in the depths of the ocean.

Reading the account of Jonah, and reflecting on the Pray4 Principle of spiritual awakening, I would argue that prayer sobers the mind in a way that nothing else can. As well as focusing the soul to a greater cause, it also reminds the human being with such incomparable force of one of life's sacred truths: we are here and now.

When we pray, we lay a marker down in the moment. Though time is constantly passing through and around us like the wind, prayer binds the seconds together with a metaphysical bench-mark. It is this realisation that we are only ever *here and now* this side of the grave, that sobers the soul. But for us to experience the sobering of the soul, we must first accept that we are out of focus to begin with. It is worth noting that the mariners were not too proud to have their minds changed, and it was *spoken prayer* that initiated this changing of the mind.

As I watched the world of Twitter become an online prayer cafe during Muamba's miraculous recovery, I – like many others – marvelled at the adaptation that was taking place virally. Web users who had often quoted the prominent atheist Richard Dawkins were now 'Praying for Muamba'. Was it all just wishful thinking? Was the

Pray4Muamba appeal just several million people trying their utmost to express their best wishes? Or did we witness a similar adaptation to that of the mariners in the Book of Jonah?

At this point I must express that I am not talking about revival or mass conversion. Indeed I do not think this is what the Pray4 Principle is about. However, conversion and prayer are intrinsically linked. I would argue that if conversion is the most important destination for the soul, 'prayer' is the pathway. This is why I feel one should never ridicule public adaptation as it moves closer to a place of true prayer.

But as we have already explored, in a culture of academic Christendom, it is difficult to accept any mass spiritual adaptation as one of genuine metaphysical change. How then should we view such adaptation? Of course we need a realistic approach. Initially, the mariners in the Book of Jonah were turning to the Lord because they had nowhere else to go. Fear, desperation and anxiety rooted their decision to corporately pray to the God of Jonah. One may argue their decision was born out of naivety. After trying the various avenues on offer, like children they tried one last means of action to get what they wanted.

But I would argue that even this spiritual naivety is something we should treat with immense respect. Does it matter what religious background or lack thereof a person has, that we might encourage or forbid them to pray? Martin Smith, author of *Compass and Stars*, unpacks this notion beautifully:

Religion is the collective sphere of our rituals and customs and observances and creeds. Religion is what we practice as members of a tribe or group with its own ethos, its mores, its calendar of observances. Spirituality is more the sphere of *why*. It concerns insight into our own unique personhood and the potential we have for an intimate relationship with the divine. Spirituality is about religion's soul and the risks of exploring the hidden roots of our behaviour and values in our fears, wounds and desires.

Throughout Jesus' ministry we see men and women from totally different spiritual upbringings adapt their perspectives to begin a prayer life. From the Jewish zealot Saul to the wayward woman at the well, Jesus' message inspires a rapid adaptation.

As it happens, the family members who sat at the bedside of Fabrice Muamba are prayerful followers of Jesus. Not only did they express their desire for the prayers of the masses, they also had the faith to go ahead and ask for them. Two God-centred national newspaper front pages, an unrivalled online prayer campaign and an international prayer request soon followed.

The potential for the human spirit to adapt to a place of prayer is one that needs contemplating. It should not only change the way we view our own Christian faith, but also how we view those willing to adapt their own position. After all, none of us were born into the correct spiritual perspective, but on the contrary, we each had to undertake our own unique version of adaptation. Like the mariners, we all had to throw caution to the wind and speak to the Lord for the first time.

## MOURN OR MOAN

Superficial, Temporary, Fashionable, Childish, Insincere, Faithless. These are some of the words I heard from the mouths of Christians describing their feelings towards the Pray4Muamba campaign. I could see why it was hard to credit the movement with uncompromising doctrinal validity. But I was also conscious of the ability we have as twenty-first-century Christians to pigeonhole aspects of secularism due to our own knee-jerk reactions. Not for a second do I think that the masses were *all* praying for the Bolton footballer. Nor do I think that those who were praying were *only* praying. But what I do believe is that almost everyone involved in the campaign was in a place of mourning. They were mourning what looked like, for a while, the sudden death of a young man in his prime.

Biblical references to the link between grief and prayer are many and varied. But I think one of the most powerful examples of prayer amid mourning comes in the opening of the Book of Nehemiah:

> The words of Nehemiah son of Hakaliah: In the month of Kislev in the twentieth year,

while I was in the citadel of Susa, Hanani, one of my brothers, came from Judah with some other men, and I questioned them about the Jewish remnant that had survived the exile, and also about Jerusalem.

They said to me, 'Those who survived the exile and are back in the province are in great trouble and disgrace. The wall of Jerusalem is broken down, and its gates have been burned with fire.'

When I heard these things, I sat down and wept. For some days I mourned and fasted and prayed before the God of heaven.

Nehemiah 1:1–4

Nehemiah was moved by a situation that did not directly affect him. He was not even living in Jerusalem at the time but, as a Jew, he felt drawn to the welfare of his people and their city. For Nehemiah, prayer and mourning were stapled together. As we saw with the mariners in the Book of Jonah, a process of adaptation took place. Nehemiah went as far as adapting his own physical position as we read that his first reaction to the troubling news was to 'sit down'. His second reaction was to weep in the citadel of Susa. The Hebrew was unconcerned with publicly showing his distress for a situation that was seemingly out of his control. And finally, he entered into a process of prayer.

*Adaptation, Appreciation, Meditation.* Before Nehemiah went on to undertake a project that would cement his name into world history, he did those three simple things. He adapted his spiritual stance with a sense of urgency, he appreciated the reality of the situation, and then launched into communication with his creator.

Public mourning and prayer are not contemporary fads invented by Twitter users. Mourning and praying have been intrinsically linked since early Jewish history. Nehemiah, Job, Isaiah, Jeremiah; the list goes on. And however tempting it is to view the reactions to Muamba's injury as an aimless online forum, we must at least show respect for the link between mourning and praying. I would argue it is quite natural to express grief and prayer simultaneously. And in a world where many would state that suffering disproves any existence of an all-powerful God, one must ask why mourning and praying still go hand in hand.

However, this pattern is not just a one-off in this generation either. Adaptation, appreciation and meditation can be seen on a corporate scale in many recent public events. Ten years after the tragic death of Diana, Princess of Wales, more than 60,000 people gathered in London's Wembley Stadium, to reflect, give thanks and pray. The Archbishop of Canterbury Dr Rowan Williams wrote specific prayers for the memorial event, which marked not only the charitable legacy left by Princess Diana, but also the aftermath of mourning felt by millions of people across the world.

One of the prayers spoken during the stadium event read:

> Father eternal, unfailing source of peace to all who seek you, we entrust to your love and protection all for whom this anniversary of the tragic and untimely death of Diana, Princess of Wales, reawakens the pains of grief and loss. Comfort all who mourn, that casting all their cares upon you, they may be filled with your gifts – of new life, of courage and of hope; through Jesus Christ our Lord. Amen.

We can clearly see echoes of Nehemiah's heart in the cries of the public during times of corporate grief like the remembrance service for Princess Diana. And, as we start to observe spiritual correlations between public grief in modern history and the ancestors of the faith, knee-jerk reactions to write off public prayer within secular circles tend to slow down.

The adaptation onboard the mariners' ship is something we should not box off as Bible only, but come to expect when suffering touches the lives of a watching world. Grief always causes the human being to adapt a certain worldly perspective. It's part of our make-up to be moved at suffering and sadness. For when we see pain, somewhere in the lining of our soul we are reminded that despite our active, thought-filled lives, we are all mere mortals. This is why prayer comes hand in hand with grief-inspired adaptation. We pray because our hope cannot be built solely on humanity, which will one day pass away, but on an immortal anchor. Without the hope of an eternal God, grief would override the human race and turn it into a cannonball of despair.

As members of the non-churchgoing public turn to prayer during times of great pain, we should, as prayerful Christians, get alongside them. When we are tempted to wear our sceptic hats, it may be more pragmatic to consciously decide to serve and encourage those who could quite possibly be praying for the first time.

Contemplating the turn of events after the Spurs vs Bolton game, I have personally asked God to change the way I view spiritual adaptation amongst those I come into contact with. I no longer see online forums or one-off remarks in favour of theism as random reactions to uncontrollable situations. Instead I try to view them as the groans of souls, who at some level, understand that all is not lost. And as I strive to become more sensitive to those in the process of adapting their religious or secular stance, I hope to become a prayerful aid myself. The question I ask when faced with the Pray4 Principle or similar spiritual awakenings is this: 'Is this person or group of people moaning or mourning. And if it's the latter, could they soon be praying?'

# 4.

# **Back to the blueprints**

*Longing desire prayeth always, though the tongue be silent. If thou art ever longing, thou art ever praying.*

Augustine

When considering the importance of prayer in a secular age and how we should engage with those seemingly outside of the faith, we must resist the temptation to muddy sound biblical advice with our own feelings and thoughts. What sits comfortably with us is not always the benchmark for biblical truth or indeed the external will of God. Of course some teaching in Scripture needs contextualising, processing and unique application. However, I would argue that when it comes to such a core faith issue as prayer, one must submit to the overarching themes displayed by God and his writers in the Bible. I know that I have too often elevated my own understanding about the application of certain Biblical teachings above the actual teaching itself. We do this for numerous reasons. Sometimes our adaptation of Scripture feels easier to share with others than the unsheathed words on the page. Often we fear that if we do present the naked message of Jesus to those outside of the faith, we will push them further away from God. But as I look at an issue like the Pray4 Principle, I believe that I have regularly gauged people's spiritual openness incorrectly. I fear the worst. The thoughts that run through my mind are something like this: 'If I intervene and offer a biblical perspective on prayer, they'll think I'm preaching.' But the truth is that offering biblical insight in an *appropriate* manner rarely comes across as invasive a way as we fear it might.

Looking back on recent history, and how prayer has played an integral public part in landmark events, we can be sure that prayer will make newspaper headlines again. So then, as well as being expectant for prayer to be juggled within secular circles, we should also be ready to input from a place of faith.

One of the key teachings on what Christian prayer should look like came early in Jesus' ministry. He addressed a large crowd who had gathered on a mountainside. I would argue that these words set a groundbreaking guide to how we should teach others to pray:

> And when you pray, do not be like the hypocrites, for they love to pray standing in the synagogues and on the street corners to be seen by others. Truly I tell you, they have received their reward in full. But when you

pray, go into your room, close the door and pray to your Father, who is unseen. Then your Father, who sees what is done in secret, will reward you. And when you pray, do not keep on babbling like pagans, for they think they will be heard because of their many words. Do not be like them, for your Father knows what you need before you ask him.

Matthew 6: 5–8

One of the reasons Jesus emphasised taking the *public* drama out of *personal* faith, was to remind a lost generation that prayer and indeed life did not revolve around them. Religion, it seems, had devolved into public ritual where one would describe a certain type of person as 'religious' and another as a 'gentile'. Today we would probably refer to the latter as secular, or maybe non-churched.

The humility, then, to pray just a few words in private oozes of confidence in something bigger than yourself. This 'quiet' style of spirituality suggests that one trusts in God whether circumstances are prosperous or disastrous. And notice that Jesus says, 'Your Father knows what you *need*' when we approach him in prayer. There is a submission that goes on in the human heart when we grapple with this subject. It is a trust that says, 'Whatever happens here, I'll continue to pray to God for the things I need'.

The exhortation to pray for Fabrice Muamba was founded on one verb, one digit and one name:

Pray4Muamba. It was a humble plea, a beautiful request and a serious suggestion. With a situation like Muamba's, one could only pray simply. My own personal prayer just hours after the incident was this: 'Father, please help Fabrice and his family. Please restore him to full health for your glory and nobody else's, in Jesus' name. Amen.'

I found myself wanting to pray for longer, to petition and struggle with the whole event, but it did not seem to fit with what Jesus teaches us in this passage. What I loved about the Twitter trend following the incident was how many people were writing their prayers as Tweets. Twitter only allows 140 characters for each post. That meant that even my short prayer wouldn't have fitted onto a Twitter feed. The prayers had to be brief, to the point, honest, without polished doctrinal charm or religious speech. Thousands wrote, 'God Help Him,' 'God Save Him,' 'God Be with Him,' 'Jesus Save Him,' 'Give Him Strength, Lord'.

We see from Jesus' teachings that God's response to prayer is never: 'Wow, I never knew that was going on, if only someone could have told me sooner!' Jesus talks about the Father as an entity that knows everyone's needs *before* they utter a word. Scanning the online forums during the preparation for this book, I must confess, I saw an air of honesty and authenticity in the prayers that may well be lacking in some religious establishments in the West. An honesty that is certainly lacking in my prayer life. The prayers were not pretty by any stretch of the imagination, but they were succinct. It is right to encourage those caught up in a prayer campaign to continue to be clear, sincere and succinct.

## MORE THAN THE ANSWER

During Luke's account of Jesus' teaching on prayer, he recorded how the teacher compared 'Father God' to a human father. This next piece of Scripture is imperative as it gives us a more accurate image of the God we are approaching in prayer. For many people outside of the faith, the image of God has been tarnished by traditional images of an old man with a beard, or an angry guy throwing lightning bolts. But as we look to encourage others to pray, we must paint as clear a picture of God as we can. Jesus said this:

> Which of you fathers, if your son asks for a fish, will give him a snake instead? Or if he asks for an egg, will give him a scorpion? If you, then, though you are evil, know how to give good gifts to your children, how much more will your Father in heaven give the Holy Spirit to those who ask him!
>
> Luke 11:11–13

We see from this teaching and in many other Gospel sermons that Jesus goes to great lengths to paint an accurate picture of God. The reasons may be obvious why Jesus would want to do such a thing, but I feel that one of his intentions was to clean up any misconceptions. Somehow, many of the non-religious folk, including the disciples, had a clouded image of who God was. They did not know how to pray (Luke 11:1), and they did not know what God was like (John 14:8). Jesus knew that one of his priorities as a teacher was to paint an accurate image of the God that had been polluted by below-par religious application.

From the teaching, we see that Jesus drives home the point that God has humankind's best intentions at heart. It is often said that God is love, and I for one am overjoyed this is true. But we also need to remind others that God is good. After all, one of the hardest truths to convey to those standing outside of the faith is that God is good despite the pain we see here in our lives.

The outpouring of thanksgiving on social networks after Muamba's recovery was massively encouraging. It is safe to say that this would not have been the case if the outcome had been different. But whatever the outcome, the Bible teaches us that God remains the same regardless. So how then do we communicate that God is a loving father even when our prayers are turned down? How do we give an accurate picture of God even when the cries of his creation are seemingly ignored?

In Philip Yancey's poignant book *Prayer: Does it Make Any Difference?*, the writer makes some great observations about God's character: 'If prayer stands as the place where God and human beings meet, then I must learn about prayer. Most of my struggles in the Christian life circle around the same two themes: why God doesn't act the way we want God to, and why I don't act the way God wants me to. Prayer is the precise point where those themes converge.'

What Yancey is arguing is that the process of prayer itself can help us all to learn more about the nature of God. And I would agree. As well as informing others about the real image of God, we must allow God to speak, or as Yancey puts it, allow God to make 'those themes converge'.

In Jesus' image of God being good, he also encourages whoever is praying to ask for the 'Holy Spirit'. In fact, this requesting for the 'Holy Spirit' seems so paramount that Jesus himself presumes it should occur in prayer generally. This notion of asking God to give the Spirit takes prayer from a place of consumerism to a place of growth. One of the key insights to biblical prayer for those starting a prayer journey is that as well as presenting our immediate requests, we should also ask God to guide us with God's Holy Spirit. It seems that Jesus pretty much guarantees that God will bless those praying with God's own character. Whether or not specific requests are met with a sovereign 'yes' from the creator, Jesus is certain that the Holy Spirit will be at work in those praying as he suggested. So the question that remains for those of us inside the faith is this: 'Would we dare to encourage those who pray to ask God specifically for God?'

If we did indeed become the sort of Christians who pointed new prayers directly to the source, not only would we be following the model of Jesus, but we would be trusting God to stand on God's 'own two feet'. This is a notion that can feel uncomfortable, as it would mean us giving up a sense of evangelistic control. But what if those in prayer do not become immediately aware of God's Spirit during prayer? What if their succinct prayers are met with an equally succinct silence? We have already seen how the Apostle Paul treated prayer as a constant ritual as opposed to a series of one-off experiences. One of the great promises in the Christian faith is that as we continue down the path of Christ we become more aware of his grace, and less dependent on our own feelings.

However, more often than not the New Testament talks about God *literally* encouraging, comforting and liberating those who engage in prayer. Paul picks up on this notion in his letter to the Church in Philippi:

> Therefore if you have any encouragement from being united with Christ, if any comfort from his love, if any common sharing in the Spirit, if any tenderness and compassion, then make my joy complete by being like-minded, having the same love, being one in spirit and of one mind.
>
> Philippians 2:1–2

This 'comfort,' 'common sharing,' 'tenderness' and 'compassion' should give us huge confidence to encourage those new to praying to rely more on God than on God's answers to any given situation. There is a pragmatism surrounding prayer that strongly suggests the more we live a life of communing with God, the more our characters will be matured by God's Holy Spirit. This is a process to which millions of Christians can testify.

Weeks after my first experience of communing with God in prayer I received many comments from friends and lecturers that my personality had been visibly affected. Many of my colleagues observed that I appeared more joyful, peaceful and hopeful. This was definitely not something I was doing on my own merit, but was indeed the work of the Holy Spirit. And like many others who have been drawn into the faith from a non-religious background, prayer seemed to be the catalyst for such sanctification.

As well as encouraging those in prayer to remember that God is good, God prioritises giving the Spirit and God can speak for God's self, we must also remember that God does not operate like us.

## UNTAMED

One of the most unhelpful temptations for Evangelicals today is to place God in a box and hand it to those outside of the Church. We take the spine of biblical doctrine and create an image of God out of our own understanding. But what we find very difficult is accounting for the part of God's character that is untamed. Wrap God up any way you want, the Bible shows us that God has always carried a trait of mystery. We know that Jesus showed us the perfect image of God in his own person, but we do not like the idea of God being spontaneous, even though Jesus himself was this very thing.

In the Old Testament we do not have to look too far to see God's wild side. Indeed, in Jesus' ministry we hear of stories when onlookers thought God was out of control. And Jesus picks up on this untamed notion when describing the Holy Spirit. In John's account, he said: 'The wind blows wherever it pleases. You hear its sound, but you cannot tell where it comes from or where it is going. So it is with everyone born of the Spirit.' (John 3:8 )

There is a place of mystery and surprise in God's character, whether we like it or not. And this is something we should not hide away from those who are not used to praying, but on the contrary, we should encourage them to embrace it. As we have already seen, God does not always give us what we want, but what we need. God is good, but not in the same way that we can be good. God is love, but not in the way that we can love. And when we approach God in prayer, we should cling to the teachings in Isaiah: ' "For my thoughts are not your thoughts, neither are your ways my ways," declares the Lord. "As the heavens are higher than the earth, so are my ways higher than your ways and my thoughts than your thoughts." ' (Isaiah 55:8 )

In C. S. Lewis's Narnia books, the author drew wonderful parallels between the character of Aslan the lion, and the Jesus of the Bible. In the eighth chapter of *The Lion, the Witch and the Wardrobe*, Mr Beaver attempts to describe what Aslan is like to Susan, one of the principal characters. She asks him: 'Is he quite safe?' As is the custom in most of C. S. Lewis's works, the writer creates an answer on two levels – one physical, one spiritual. Mr Beaver replies: 'Who said anything about safe? 'Course he isn't safe. But he's good.'

This epic idea that something so wild can also be so good is one that helps us describe what God is like to those starting out in prayer. God always leads God's followers out of their comfort zone. Reading through some of David's psalms gives us a great picture of how God often delays a response from the point of the King's first prayer. And so it is with Jesus. Some people have an image of Jesus that is out of balance with what the Bible presents. Some see Jesus as a halo-wearing angel figure who pats us on the head when we are struggling. Others see God as a menace, moving the goalposts of our lives. However, it is important to hold two key paradoxes together: God is good, God is untamed.

Another helpful picture is drawn in the final chapter of C. S. Lewis's *The Lion the Witch and the Wardrobe* as Aslan walks away without making a fuss during the celebrations. Again, Mr Beaver addresses the children: 'He'll be coming and going … One day you'll see him and another you won't. He doesn't like being tied down—and of course he has other countries to attend to … He'll drop in often … He's wild, you know. Not like a tame lion.'

The important lessons to encourage those new to prayer are simple and inclusive. Prayer should be vulnerable and honest, but anchored with the conscious understanding that God is both good and wild. One must also hold onto Jesus' teaching that prayer is not just listing requirements but actually engaging with Father God and Son Jesus through the power of the Holy Spirit, who is given to those who ask for him.

We must remember that as much as prayer is a verb, it is also a place. It is a place where spiritually blind mortal beings can access the love and wild grace of an immortal God. As an athlete goes to the training venue to grow in strength, we go to a place of prayer to grow in grace. But as we encourage others to trust this good and wild God during prayer, we must also trust this good and wild God with them individually.

# 5.

# Fabrice Muamba

In the summer of 2012, the Christian men's magazine *Sorted* published an interview with Fabrice Muamba about the events of his heart attack on 17 March that year, the public response and his own thoughts about prayer. Fabrice, who has overcome some incredibly challenging situations throughout his life already, answered the questions honestly, vulnerably and passionately. With the kind permission of Fabrice and *Sorted*, extracts from the interview are published here.*

*Looking back on the event, what was the last thing you can remember?*
I just felt my normal self before the game and I was fine up until it happened. I was full of energy and I felt normal and fighting fit. It was just a normal match. When it happened, it was strange. There was no sign of it coming. I felt a bit dizzy just before, but

---

* For context, the interviewer's original questions are printed in bold. The reproduction of extracts from this interview does not indicate Fabrice Muamba's endorsement of *The #Pray4 Principle* or his agreement with its content

it didn't feel like you normally do when you feel dizzy, it was different. It was like having an out-of-body experience, like I was running alongside my own body. It was surreal.

It was at that point that I started to see double. It was so strange, like a dream. I knew something was wrong when I looked up and I saw two Scott Parkers. David Wheater, our defender, was shouting at me to get back and help out. He obviously didn't know what was happening to me, but then again neither did I. It was then I just fell through the air and with two big bumps of my head I hit the ground right in front of me. And that was it, there was nothing; there was just blackness. I was dead.

*What are your memories after the darkness?*
When I woke up I was lying in hospital with loads of wires inside me. It was scary. It was really scary.

I remember I could hear people praying. My family was praying next to me and I was lying there in bed. And when I moved my fingers for the first time, I was still in a strange place. I was thinking, 'Why am I here?' I wasn't sure what had happened.

The incident happened on the Saturday; I was out until the Monday. When I woke up, I didn't know where I was and Shauna, my fiancée, had to tell me what had happened to me. I couldn't believe it! I said: 'To me? Are you serious?' I had to steady myself, to take a moment. It was surreal.

But then my immediate concern was whether my family was okay – and the score of the game I was playing in! I actually asked if we had lost or not.

*How do you feel when looking back at the event?*
It was scary to hear what had happened, but instantly I knew someone had been there looking out for me. I am sure that I was being watched. It was a miracle; it was more than a miracle. It was only on the morning of the game that my father and I had a prayer together. We asked God to protect me and He did. He didn't let me down when I needed Him. I am walking proof of the power of prayer.

I was dead for 78 minutes. It is incredible. And even if I survived, everybody thought I would have brain damage. But I am alive and I am fine. It is incredible.

God works in mysterious ways, I believe that. That doctor had to be in the stadium, it was amazing. I think he was one of God's angels. When I left the hospital, he admitted he hadn't been convinced I would ever leave; he didn't think it was going to happen. And he said I should be brain damaged. I am so grateful.

*Many young athletes do not survive cardiac arrests. Marc Vivien-Foe and Piermario Morosini both died following the same injury. How does this affect your perspective now?*
I thank God every single day that I am alive, and so does my family. My mum, my fiancée, my son – we all pray to God and thank him that I am still here. I can get emotional about this because I know I was gone; I shouldn't be here. But with God's will, I am.

It is important to have God on your side. If God is with me, then who can be against me? That is I how I see it. That's always a mantra I have lived by, and is certainly one that will stay with me. How could it not?

[Speaking about the recent death of Piermario Morosini] That was hard for me to see. It was hard for me to take, because what happened to him happened to me. I could imagine what happened to him. But I survived and he didn't.

## How do you think the prayers of the people helped you?

People were sending me and my fiancée messages through the internet, telling us they were praying. I felt all those prayers. They definitely helped me. In times of need we always turn to God, or for non-Christians an omnipresent being. For me it was a testament to how strong God's power is and how we lean on Him in times of need.

It's a daily part of my routine. I pray regardless of if I'm overcoming problems or having great success and achievements. Praying to God expresses a gratitude for how fortunate we are and I've always found comfort in prayer.

I pray on a daily basis for my family, health and prosperity. As the Bible says, 'He who started this good work will carry it to the end'.

It's true, my memory isn't great. I repeat myself quite a bit and can't remember things like I used to be able to, but I am still healing, and I am okay with that. I'm a huge believer in the power of prayer and I know it helped my recovery process. It's the central part of my life and I know prayer heals, so for me it helped me mentally, spiritually and physically.

*Why do you think God answers some prayers with 'yes' and others 'no'?*
I am really not sure, perhaps to reconfirm faith in believers. I believe we all have to walk a path and what happened to me is mine.

I knew my immediate family prayed for me and they also told me and showed me the prayers and support that I received worldwide. It was over-whelming and I say thank you every day for those people who did: the people in the crowd, other football fans and players, and everyone else who did so. I am very, very grateful.

If what happened to me has helped all of us come together a bit more and remind us how fantastic and supportive this nation is, then maybe it is worth it. The support of everyone has been such a great help. The support has been incredible, and I am just happy to still be here. I can walk freely and that feels like such a gift. Bolton is a special football club; it is a special place to be and to play football. And the club has been fantastic to me … and that is everyone: the staff, the players and, of course, the supporters. But it is not just those from Bolton; the support has come from everywhere around the country. I got so many cards. I am so grateful and happy. When I read them, I have to take a moment. It was overwhelming, it still is, and I appreciate it every single day.

*What does life look like for you now?*
After you have been in hospital like I have, you are grateful just to be able to do easy things, like walking around. I was happy when I got out just to have a bit of freedom.

I now have two hearts. The new one can kick-start the old one if a cardiac arrest was to happen again. I had a choice of where I could put the new heart, so I thought up near my shoulder, near to my old heart, would be the best place. So, with two hearts, I don't know whether or not I'll be able to play football again. With the grace of God, I hope to be back on the pitch, but really it is not important. Wherever the Lord wants my life to go, my dream is to play again. I have a determination to do that but it is not an overnight process. Football is a career – one I love and which has been very good to me and my family – [but]loving and worshipping Christ has always been how I live my life.

I appreciate life more and I no longer walk with fear as I know who my living saviour is. I will look to spread the Word of God and what he has done for my life.

*What does the future hold for you?*
At the moment, I just want to make sure I recover as best I can. That is what I want to concentrate on. I just want to spend time with my family and watch my son grow up. Just to be able to hold him again – there is no money in the world that can buy that. That is important to me, because I was dead for 78 minutes. So I'm just taking my time.

'People should believe in miracles. If you don't believe in miracles, look at me. I am a walking miracle. It's beyond a miracle. It is God's power.'

Fabrice Muamba, speaking to *Sorted*, August 2012

Fabrice went on to explain that his life goals now included getting married to his fiancée and returning to the game. However, despite reaching a miraculous level of fitness, good enough to carry the Olympic torch around east London in the build-up to the London 2012 Olympics, Fabrice announced his retirement from the game later in August. The decision came after specialist doctors in Belgium advised him on his future participation in the sport. Speaking in August, he said:

Since suffering my heart attack and being discharged from hospital, I have remained utterly positive in the belief I could one day resume my playing career and play for Bolton Wanderers once again.

As part of my ongoing recovery, last week I travelled to Belgium to seek further medical advice from a leading cardiologist. But the news I received was obviously not what I had hoped it would be and it means I am now announcing my retirement from professional football.

Despite Fabrice showing natural signs of great sadness after being forced into early retirement, he continued to display a familiar sense of grace and thankfulness:

> Football has been my life since I was a teenage boy and it has given me so many opportunities. Above all else, I love the game and count myself very lucky to have been able to play at the highest level.

Football Association Chairman David Bernstein was one of the first to respond to Fabrice's announcement. He said: 'His recovery has been miraculous and a great tribute to all who have been involved. I would like to wish him the very best for the future and I know that the thoughts of the entire football family will be with him.'

Like all viral campaigns, the Pray4Muamba one was relatively short-lived. It came to a halt as soon as Fabrice had been given a clean bill of health and subsequently retired from the game. However, with the forum being online, anyone can revisit the hundreds of thousands of comments left by prayerful onlookers who submitted their thoughts and prayers throughout the ordeal.

During the replayed fixture between Bolton and Spurs, Fabrice Muamba made an emotional return to the Reebok Stadium. He was welcomed by a standing ovation from both sets of fans who passionately chanted the name 'Fabrice Muamba'. Fabrice stood in the centre of the pitch and wept with appreciation for the support from the football world who paved the way for the Pray4Muamba campaign.

On his return to the Bolton faithful, Muamba paid tribute to those who supported him in front of national media. He testified to having boxes full of messages that had been sent to him and that he was truly overwhelmed by the response of the watching world.

Following Fabrice Muamba's retirement, the websites that so effectively covered the Pray4Muamba campaign were once again flooded with comments. It was typical of the campaign to see those from different religious and non-religious backgrounds paying tribute to Fabrice, the medical experts and the faith of the Muamba family. Inevitably there were comments challenging any divine intervention surrounding the campaign, but overall a sense of unity was displayed around the notion that something incredible had happened.

Throughout the recovery process, the return to the Reebok Stadium and the retirement, Fabrice Muamba was commended for his humility, grace and determination.

Personally, I was honoured to witness prayerful unity within secular society. Like so many people I was privileged to play a tiny part in the Pray4Muamba campaign. There is no doubt that lives were changed by the spiritual outpouring that followed.

## THE FOLLOWING COMMENTS WERE PUBLISHED BY MEMBERS OF THE PUBLIC ON THE BBC SPORT WEBSITE IN AUGUST 2012:

Whether you believe God saved him or not, Muamba was dead for 74 minutes. That's the closest thing to a miracle I've ever seen. I wish him nothing but the best.

Dr Heath

A little sad but your health must always come first. As for who or what saved his life. The man himself gives thanks to his medical team but believes his faith was instrumental in his recovery. Secularists have no business belittling his faith or anybody else's. Good luck to him.

OldWoodman

The incident has been represented with dignity, warmth and respect, and all of these characteristics are present in his announcement today. He will be missed but never forgotten at Bolton.

Anonymous

I have followed Fabrice's story with great fascination, being a nurse, and with great pride in the profession that restored him to us. If he cannot return to football, he accepts it with good grace, as should we. I wish him a happy and healthy 'retirement' and the hope that his future life will be long and rewarding. Bon chance, Fabrice.

Chris Olsen

Truly, one of God's greatest creations. Fabrice Muamba.

Bolton_00

As a British/Irish man in the Congo, it makes me very sad that Fabrice Muamba has been forced to retire on medical advice. However, I am very happy that Fabrice is still with us and I am sure he can find a purpose for the rest of his long life. The one thing that strikes me about what happened to him is the goodwill that seemed to exist between all football fans at that time. FM, merci pour tous.

SimonInCongo

# 6.

# **Godly expectations**

One of the first specific prayers I uttered after finding faith, aged 16, was for a girl I was totally in love with to find it in her heart to love me. We were already friends, both active in the Church and deemed a 'great couple' by onlookers. I remember reading Matthew 7:7 repeatedly: 'Ask and it will be given to you; seek and you will find; knock and the door will be opened to you.' For months I prayed for nothing else.

When it came to approaching the subject directly with her, despite being full of faith, the conversation didn't go as planned. This particular young woman did not feel any attraction to me in that way. I remember feeling a definite sense of anger towards God. I had prayed earnestly and worked out with my own sound logic that we should have been an item. Looking back on the state of my then infant faith, however, I can say this: I had great expectations, but no godly assumptions. My heart's desire was to be loved by someone I really cared for. My logic was based purely on what I was feeling at the time. Today

I can testify that the young woman in the story is married to a man who suits her far better than I ever could. This is a case of my not having my prayers granted turning out for the better.

One of the hardest lessons I've had to learn since my encounter with the Christian message is not to second-guess God. During the heartache of being rejected in love, I constantly believed that the creator of all things was either out of their mind or just persecuting me. I second-guessed the will of God for my life.

It does not take a genius to work out that God is often being kind to say 'no' to some of our blind prayers. However, the boundaries begin to blur when the situation is not based solely on selfish desires. Praying for someone involved in a natural disaster or for the safety of a child who has been kidnapped; these are the prayer requests that should surely be on God's agenda? How do we approach this subject for our own lives and the lives of those praying in secular society?

Right from the off I would argue that as important as prayer should be, living with godly expectations shoud be equally so. We need to have some idea of what we *could* and *should* expect when we approach God in prayer. After all, we are not approaching a God who has not revealed their character to us, for in Christ we see exactly what God the Father is like. (John 14:7)

One of the stories in Jesus' ministry that often gets overlooked is the fascinating prayer request of the centurion. The encounter depicts a great example of how faith and prayer are linked. Luke writes about a centurion's much-needed servant who was about to die. The centurion heard that Jesus was in the area and asked for a message to be delivered to him to come and pray for his servant. Jesus set off and headed towards the centurion's house when something incredible happened:

> He was not far from the house when the centurion sent friends to say to him:
>
> 'Lord, don't trouble yourself, for I do not deserve to have you come under my roof. That is why I did not even consider myself worthy to come to you. But say the word, and my servant will be healed. For I myself am a man under authority, with soldiers under me. I tell this one, "Go," and he goes; and that one, "Come," and he comes. I say to my servant, "Do this," and he does it.'
>
> When Jesus heard this, he was amazed at him, and turning to the crowd following him, he said, 'I tell you, I have not found such great faith even in Israel.' Then the men who had been sent returned to the house and found the servant well.
>
> Luke 7: 6–10

It seems from this account that humility, faith and prayer have become woven into the centurion's character. What strikes me as integral within this story is that a person of faith can actually *amaze* Jesus. The centurion had worked out that it didn't matter how or where a specific prayer took place, the important truth was that Jesus is sovereign. This lesson is both liberating and challenging. We are liberated at the knowledge that we can approach Christ at any point of our daily lives, but then challenged at how we often rely on religious traditions and establishments to pray at all.

One could also suggest that from the example of the centurion that faith is not just beneficial to prayer, but it can at times be very necessary. At this juncture we must be careful how we adopt the centurion's example in our own prayer life; for even the notion of faith is something we may see differently to how God sees it. What we might recognise as faithfulness may actually be over-optimistic hope. Someone who expresses a great desire for something might actually have very little faith. We see that the centurion displayed the authenticity of his faith by humbly accepting that Jesus could deploy his kingdom from any point in space and time.

So if faith and prayer are linked, how then should these attributes develop godly expectations within us? I would suggest that a godly expectation is one that is sincere but not demanding. Another great model for godly expectation can be found in the book of Daniel.

## EVEN IF

During the rule of King Nebuchadnezzar, a decree was issued legally binding everyone in the region to fall down and worship a golden image in Babylon at certain points of the day. This decree directly compromised the Jewish faith, which prohibited the worship of idols. At the time, three Jews called Shadrach, Meshach and Abednego refused to obey the King's command. We pick the story up after the King summoned the three and threatened them with execution in a blazing furnace.

> Shadrach, Meshach and Abednego replied to him, 'King Nebuchadnezzar, we do not need to defend ourselves before you in this matter. If we are thrown into the blazing furnace, the God we serve is able to deliver us from it, and he will deliver us from Your Majesty's hand. But even if he does not, we want you to know, Your Majesty, that we will not serve your gods or worship the image of gold you have set up.'
> Daniel 3:16–18

For me, this is arguably one of the greatest examples of godly assumption aside from Jesus' example at Gethsemane. We see three men faced with the imminent threat of death eager to proclaim the potential power of God. Note they did not assume that God would definitely intervene; neither did they attempt to prayerfully manipulate their creator. They boldly proclaimed that, regardless of God's direct intervention, none of them would compromise their faith. This is a lesson we must look to instil in our lives as well those praying within secular circles. As Philip Yancey puts it in his very helpful book *Disappointment with God*, 'We tend to think, "Life should be fair because God is fair." But God is not life. And if I confuse God with the physical reality of life – by expecting constant good health for example--then I set myself up for crashing disappointment.'

A person of faith must be one who does not assume God's next move. From both examples in Scripture we can safely say that God's ideal for a mature prayer is one that admits two key truths: 1) God can do anything; 2) God might do nothing.

But as we reflect on the faith of the three Jewish friends in the book of Daniel, one could argue that God's response to our prayers may be irrelevant in the bigger picture. For years I believed the bigger picture for my Christian walk was for me to pray about everything until I worked out God's specific will for my life. And in doing this, I would somehow learn how to pray for things that God would definitely answer positively. But we see from many of Paul's letters to the believers in the early church that this is not the bigger picture for our lives. God does not state that God's will is for us to master the art of praying 'no brainers' and hitting a spiritual purple streak. Paul holds nothing back when discussing God's will for our lives in his letter to the Colossian church:

For this reason, since the day we heard about you, we have not stopped praying for you. We continually ask God to fill you with the knowledge of his will through all the wisdom and understanding that the Spirit gives, so that you may live a life worthy of the Lord and please him in every way: bearing fruit in every good work, growing in the knowledge of God, being strengthened with all power according to his glorious might so that you may have great endurance and patience, and giving joyful thanks to the Father, who has qualified you to share in the inheritance of his people in the kingdom of light.

Colossians 1:9–12

What you'll notice quite clearly is that Paul does not suggest that God's will is for us to get everything we pray for, but that we would develop a *knowledge* and *understanding* of God through our faith. With this in mind, it is imperative that when we engage with those beginning to pray, we remind them that prayer is not about the task at hand, but developing trust in the God at hand.

Paul stipulates that one of the aims we should adopt as personal targets is to develop 'great endurance' and 'patience' in the Christian faith. The question one must ask on the back of these targets is, if we were people who got everything we prayed for, the need for 'great endurance' and 'patience' would be redundant.

We cannot negotiate the truths around godly assumptions without looking at the most godly man to grace humanity with his presence: Jesus. Just 24 hours before his death, we can find the Nazarene praying with perfect humility and profound vulnerability:

> Jesus went out as usual to the Mount of Olives, and his disciples followed him. On reaching the place, he said to them, 'Pray that you will not fall into temptation'. He withdrew about a stone's throw beyond them, knelt down and prayed, 'Father, if you are willing, take this cup from me; yet not my will, but yours be done.' An angel from heaven appeared to him and strengthened him. And being in anguish, he prayed more earnestly, and his sweat was like drops of blood falling to the ground.
>
> Luke 22:39–44

If anyone was worthy of assuming whatever he saw fit, it was Jesus. Yet even in his darkest hour, Jesus prayed those benchmark words, 'Not my will, but yours be done'.

Reflecting on my interview with Fabrice Muamba, I was astonished at how he does not look at his miraculous recovery with a sense of over-familiarity, but on the contrary, sees it as an example of God's grace. His thankfulness to God for giving him more time with his loved ones is evident. There is no doubt that Muamba believes it was God's will for him to live, but not once did Muamba assume that he had an automatic right to life itself.

Jesus epitomises this humble trait as he submitted to God's final word on the situation. Though part of our fallen, human state longs to assume we know why God allows certain things to happen or not happen in our lives, we are told to follow in the example of Jesus and develop godly assumptions.

So what can we assume then? I would argue that from the models set by Christ, the Jews in the furnace and the centurion, are threefold: 1) God hears us; 2) God loves us; 3) God wants the best thing for us.

Whatever the seriousness or the seemingly unimportant nature of our prayers, a godly assumption would be that our heavenly Father hears our words. This assumption is vital as we look to engage with prayer in secular society. When faced with the questions of God's omnipotence, one can encourage others that God is always listening. This should come as great news for a searching soul. The centurion took solace in knowing Jesus did not have to be physically close to him for a prayer to be effective. And with that in mind we can encourage others that regardless of how close they feel to God physically, sincere prayer is valid. This is also good news for us already following Jesus. We can be assured that the validity of our prayers does not depend on the comfort within our circumstance.

The second godly assumption we can adopt is that God loves us. One of my favourite aspects to Jesus' personality is how he looked on crowds of regular folk with compassion. During his early ministry Jesus looked on a random group of locals before making a beautiful and poignant observation: 'When he saw the crowds, he had compassion on them, because they were harassed and helpless, like sheep without a shepherd. Then he said to his disciples, "The harvest is plentiful but the workers are few. Ask the Lord of the harvest, therefore, to send out workers into his harvest field." '

Matthew 9:36–38

Jesus has compassion for us. Though this is a fundamental truth that has anchored the Christian faith throughout generations, it is one we quite often forget when we pray. But as we contemplate how we encourage those taking their first steps of prayer, it is important that we remind others that God does not just love us, but he is indeed *love*. (1 John 4:8)

And the third assumption that I would argue one can adopt before, during and after prayer, is that God's plan for our lives is better than our own. This is arguably the hardest lesson to apply to prayer. Time and time again we are faced with painful situations, seemingly void of God's intervention, yet the Bible reminds us that God knows best. Or as C. S. Lewis put it: 'We're not necessarily doubting that God will do the best for us; we are wondering how painful the best will turn out to be.'

As we learn to trust God with our daily lives we are in effect turning away from our own understanding.

The act of admitting that God's will is better for us, despite the painful process of character development, will lead us into a far more liberating existence. For if we learn to cast our anxieties on God, we begin to operate out of a place of faith, and not fear.

There are times when we feel drawn to pray for specific things. This sense of calling can then be mixed with passion and prayerful fervour. But even during these times, we must reflect soberly on the truth that God does not answer prayers solely because we feel they are the best option for our lives or the lives of those around us. After all, God did not take the cup away from Jesus, the son of God, but allowed him to be crucified. And Jesus himself did not heal every sick person in his vicinity but focused on a number of individuals and groups. However, there is great reassurance that God promises the best option for us in our blind lives. As we accept that God did not release Jesus from his horrific execution, we simultaneously see God's master plan for the salvation of the world through the events at Calvary.

In Paul's letter to the Colossian Church, we see for us to learn of God's will for our lives, we must be filled with knowledge from God. We know that this knowledge is accessed through God's Word, the Bible, and his Spirit. The great news is that these tools are at hand for those praying today as they were for those praying in the upper room. And the three godly assumptions we have considered are truths that were brought to life before the foundations of the world. As it says:

For you know that it was not with perishable things such as silver or gold that you were redeemed from the empty way of life handed down to you from your ancestors, but with the precious blood of Christ, a lamb without blemish or defect. He was chosen before the creation of the world, but was revealed in these last times for your sake. Through him you believe in God, who raised him from the dead and glorified him, and so your faith and hope are in God.

1 Peter 1:18–21

God hears us
God loves us
God wants the best thing for us.

# 7.

# **Godly reactions**

> The more carefully and frequently you
> monitor yourself, the better you'll control
> yourself.
>
> Roy Baumeister

No child refuses to eat food ever again on the
account that his parents would not allow him or her
to eat a whole chocolate cake ten minutes before
bedtime. There may be tears and unwarranted accu-
sations from the child, but you can bet your mort-
gage that he or she will eat again the next morning.
To refuse to eat again because one thing did not go
your way would be a reaction founded in insanity. It
would be a reaction destined to harm the one in
question.

As we consider the notion of developing godly
reactions to sincerely spoken prayers, we must speak
honestly about the temptation to react badly when
things do not go our way. As humans we all harbour
the ability to cut off our noses to spite our faces.
Selfish reactions to unanswered prayers or compro-

mised hope will affect every human at one stage in our lives. We are prone to pick a fight with God; whether it be an all out screaming session, or an internal spat. Selfishness laces our DNA. As Jane Austen once said, 'Selfishness must always be forgiven you know, because there is no hope of a cure.'

How do we fight our negative spirits that so effectively persuade us that God is in the wrong if our lives do not match up to the ones in our daydreams? Or on the contrary, how does one respond when our prayers do get answered? Is there a model for godly reactions to earthly situations?

## REACTIONS TO PAIN

He was the greatest man among all the people of the East. He was upright, he was holy, he was honest and everyone thought highly of him. In one tragic event he lost his sons, his daughters, his employees and his business; his name was Job. When the news of the fateful day reached Job's ears, his reaction became legend. He may have been excused for going on an all-night drinking session or fleeing the country. Some may have expected him to descend into a place of severe depression or unstoppable anger, but not Job:

> At this, Job got up and tore his robe and shaved his head. Then he fell to the ground in worship and said: 'Naked I came from my mother's womb. And naked I shall depart. The

Lord gave and the Lord has taken away; may the name of the Lord be praised.

1 Job 20–21

The thought of a man responding to arguably the worst news possible, with prayer and worship, seems almost crass. But what we see in Job's account is not a man disguising pain with pious rhetoric, but a man who knew how to react well. The whole book of Job goes on to explore the internal wrestling and examination of faith inside a godly man. But in his turmoil and struggle we see a guy who had learned to be *honest* with God, without compromising God in the process.

It is this honesty that I would like to explore. Was Job in a place of mourning? Yes, of course, for we see how he shaved his head and tore his clothes in an act of grief. From this we can safely assume that a godly reaction to tragedy, or unanswered prayer, should be as honest as possible. In fact, if there is one thing we can learn from the prayers of the spiritual leaders in the Old Testament, it is this: God is big enough to handle our honesty.

Around two years ago I was visiting a friend in a local church in North Yorkshire. He had been appointed as a leader of the congregation and I popped across the Moors to encourage him in his new role. During the service I saw a man sitting in the front pew of the church dressed very fashionably. He was unshaven with messy hair, and was in his late 30s. His eyes were bloodshot to such an extent I thought he may have had an infection. But as the service went on, I watched this man weep constantly. During the time of sung worship at the end of the service, he was on his knees, mumbling the same two words over and over again. Amid the lyrics 'I will sing of your love forever,' this man was mumbling: 'Why, God?'

My friend sat next to the man for the entirety of the worship and never once took his arm off his shoulder. I could see members of the church place their hands on him as they walked up for communion. Over coffee that afternoon, my friend informed me that the man's name was Oliver and he had recently lost his 35-year-old wife to cancer. He had two young children. What I saw was a man bare his soul to his creator, regardless of the quaint setting of an old North Yorkshire church.

I spent weeks reflecting on both Oliver's situation and reaction, and I became aware that in many churches, small groups, community clubs, pubs and places of work, I seldom allowed people space to bare their souls. I certainly did not encourage people to express the more vulnerable emotions in the depths of their lives. And though we know a church full of grief would not provide an ideal environment for growth, we must recognise that grief is something that will be affecting every member of the congregation at some point in their lives. I would argue that grieving *honestly* is not just a valid reaction to life's imminent hardship, but also a healthy one; and definitely godly.

When engaging with those outside of the faith who testify to unanswered prayers or unjustified suffering, we must also remember the emotion of Christ. One of the sad results following centuries of polished, established Christianity is that the person of Christ has become one that does not always match up to the man we find in Scripture. Images of Jesus portrayed in the media and in church memorabilia often show a man devoid of emotion, seemingly unaffected by life around him. Unfortunately, this image has transcended to the secular mindset where many non-believers describe Jesus as a 'nice' man or a 'quiet' teacher.

But as soon as we brush the surface of the accounts of Jesus' ministry we see a man who was not afraid to react honestly, vulnerably and passionately to suffering. One of the most moving instances in the New Testament accounts is recorded as the shortest verse in the Bible. It confirms the argument that an emotional reaction to a sad or challenging situation is one that can also be godly.

Jesus was heading to the tomb of Martha's brother Lazarus. The community was in mourning at the passing of Lazarus and Jesus met with the dead man's sister where he claimed he could raise him from the grave. There was an air of frustration around the scene where people were commenting, 'If only Jesus had been here when Lazarus died'. The story explains:

> Now Jesus had not yet entered the village, but was still at the place where Martha had met

him. When the Jews who had been with Mary in the house, comforting her, noticed how quickly she got up and went out, they followed her, supposing she was going to the tomb to mourn there.

When Mary reached the place where Jesus was and saw him, she fell at his feet and said, 'Lord, if you had been here, my brother would not have died.'

When Jesus saw her weeping, and the Jews who had come along with her also weeping, he was deeply moved in spirit and troubled. 'Where have you laid him?' he asked.

'Come and see, Lord,' they replied.

Jesus wept.

Then the Jews said, 'See how he loved him!' But some of them said, 'Could not he who opened the eyes of the blind man have kept this man from dying?' Jesus, once more deeply moved, came to the tomb. It was a cave with a stone laid across the entrance. 'Take away the stone,' he said.

John 11:30–39

What I have always found deeply fascinating about this account is that Jesus knew he had the power and the intention to raise Lazarus from the dead. But despite knowing fully that he was about to turn the people's mourning into joy, he was still moved to tears before the resurrection. It begs the question, why did Jesus weep when he knew the story had a happy ending?

I would argue that Jesus, being both completely human and completely Lord modelled to us a pattern of behaviour in which we can both empathise and ultimately follow. Godly reactions to bad news do not have to be controlled, succinct prayers. There are situations in our lives that justify the tearing of robes, the shaving of heads and public weeping. If we do not encourage people to be honest with their creator in prayer, why encourage them to pray at all?

## GRIEVE AND BELIEVE

Recently I attended the funeral of an elderly lady who died on the south coast of England. Though I have attended numerous funerals, this was the first overtly 'Christian' service I had been to. By that I mean the lady who had died was an active part of the local church and regularly professed faith in Jesus.

I was taken back by the drastically different atmosphere in the room. Though there were clear signs of sadness scattered throughout the church, there was an evident sense of a greater peace. The language people used was one of hope and, in some circumstances, joy. I chatted with the church leader about his experiences in 'Christian' and 'secular' funerals, and how the congregations react to the event, and he summed it up in poignant fashion. He said: 'When the process of death is void of hope, there seems to be a sting in the air. But where there is faith, there seems to be no sting at all.'

Jesus modelled a reaction of honest emotion, but not at the expense of belief. It is this balance that I would like to explore further.

Going back to the story of Job, you may know that Job's life fell into more sadness after the initial experience of losing his family members, servants and business. For Job, there came a process of honest searching and questioning. Philosophical conversations between him and a group of thinkers took place in an attempt to rationalise the grief, but to no avail.

We see the story climax when the Lord speaks directly with Job. In a monologue that would humble the most modest of men, the Lord reminds Job of how blind the eyes of the mortal really are.

For everyone reacting to sadness or disappointment, as Job did, there will always be the temptation to give oneself over to grief. The Lord knew this was possible for Job, and intervened to remind his faithful servant of the importance of belief as well as grief. In response to the Lord's humbling sovereign reminder, Job uttered these important words:

> I am unworthy – how can I reply to you? I put my hand over my mouth. I spoke once, but I have no answer – twice, but I will say no more.

> Job 40:4–5

What strikes me in Job's response to the Lord is the ability he has to leave his initial raw response of grief in the hands of God. He knows there is a temptation to lose his daily life to an existence of constant complaint, but he refuses to live there. In fact he allows his mouth the freedom to express frustration, anger and raw emotion once, but as he says at the end of the verse: 'Twice, but I will say no more'.

Youth worker Nick Welford, based in the North East of England, once delivered a series of seminars on the issue of dedicating a specific time to grieve honestly with God, but not dwelling in the season on grief itself. Commenting on Job's 'Speak once' method, he said: 'We have to ask ourselves if Job's approach could work in our culture? Could we get our complaint out of our system for a season and then strive to put our hands over our mouth in awe and reverence before God? Could we complain, shout or argue once or twice, before agreeing that it might be time to stop?'

It is a hard notion to grapple with, especially in a culture which urges the general public to follow their heart at all costs. But coming to God in prayer, as previously discussed, is a symbolic confession that states that we are not God, and our spiritual development is one that God should lead, not us. As we engage with those beginning to pray, we must remind them that God's plan for our character growth is one of godly motion. It is this motion that prevents our grief stagnating both our thought life and our soul life. Very rarely does God want us to stand still in our lives, but to grow in the knowledge and understanding of God's will. But though he does not want us to *stand* still, it does not mean he does not want us to *be* still.

## PRAY THROUGH THE GEARS

How do we know when a season of complaint has come to an end? When does the 'Speak once' become 'Speak twice'? How can we discern when our honest prayers of grief have become simply stagnating?

The truth is there is no method of discernment to pinpoint when we need to move on in prayer. All of us, unique in design, face unique emotional and spiritual states continuously. But there are great methods we can put in place to help discern when our prayer life, and subsequently our state of mind, needs to move from a place of pause to a place of progress.

One of the key assets to the notion of prayer is that it is not just a singular stream of communication, but a universal tool. Praying with others is a hugely beneficial act and one that provides great growth for all involved. When hearing someone talk about their new experiences of prayer, we could, as followers of Jesus, offer to pray with them. Though Jesus overtly encouraged an individual style of prayer behind closed doors, (Matthew 6:6) we also hear Jesus speaking of a corporate prayer later on in the same gospel account: 'Again, truly I tell you that if two of you on earth agree about anything they ask for, it will be done for them by my Father in heaven. For where two or three gather in my name, there am I with them.' (Matthew 18:19–20 )

Godly reactions can be encouraged and shaped much more easily when you are praying alongside someone new to the notion of prayer. From a distance, it is easy to make assumptions on how someone can grow in the faith, but when praying side by side, the process becomes far more personal. Accountability is an extremely helpful signpost to developing godly assumptions and mature reactions.

Another tool to keep new prayers moving in a godly direction is to pray with a specific Bible verse or chapter in mind. It might feel strange to encourage a prayerful newcomer to open the Bible during their initial stages of faith, but scripture both anchors and directs prayer, regardless of the maturity of those praying.

And finally, as we look to engage with those praying in a secular culture, we might encourage them to keep a prayer journal. This would be a very simple diary of what prayers were spoken and any revelations or specific streams of thought that were present during the prayer time. Journaling allows those in prayer to review and mediate on the weeks, months and years that pass. The journal itself becomes a visible reminder of where the individual has come from, and a good indicator to where they are heading.

Overall, the message that I have been most encouraged by during my eleven years as someone who prays, is that faith is about longevity and not just spontaneity. Prayer was not created to be used to shine briefly, like the last lights of a shooting star. Prayer is the glue to a spiritual journey that is meant to last the whole of this life and beyond. We need to be encouraging those praying around us that it is more important that we finish this earthly experience with prayer still on our lips rather than merely in our memories. Prayer should inspire godly assumptions, godly reactions and godly living. Like our faith, prayer was built to last.

# 8.

# Moving the starting line

> We tend to use prayer as a last resort, but God
> wants it to be our first line of defence. We pray
> when there's nothing else we can do, but God
> wants us to pray before we do anything at all.
> Oswald Chambers

In a response to some concerning church attendance
statistics in the latter part of the twentieth century, a
vast array of starting points for new Christians began
to sprout up in the UK. During the early 1990s the
Alpha course became hugely popular throughout
many churches, seeing great results in church
growth. In more recent years churches have adopted
similar introductory programmes including Christianity Explored and the Emmaus Discipleship
Course. And though there are now several starting
lines for hearing and experiencing the message of
Jesus, the model for each idea is a carbon copy of the
previous one. In short, a group of people are invited
to a series of events hosted by a church where they
can process the message of a speaker, discuss the

nuances of Christ's claims and ideally come to a decision to take the calling of Jesus more seriously.

I can testify personally to the great work carried out on these introductory courses. As well as making great friends on Alpha groups I helped lead, I also had the privilege of seeing my friends come to a place of faith during the course. But as I engage with the ever-changing culture of secularism, I believe we may have to look again at creating a new space or method to help searchers experience the message of Jesus. Notions of intellectual debate, philosophical processing and conversations over a three-course meal seem to suit a certain social group. Many of the men and women with whom I attend my local pub have painted broad brushstrokes over introductory Christian courses deeming them 'middle class' or 'posh'. Now I know from experience this is not the case, but I am fascinated by how even this *style* of course can give off a certain appearance to many outside of the church.

## REALITY VERSUS TRUTH

The cross-denominational dwindling church attendances in the UK, courtesy of wide media coverage, are no secret. And despite our passion to communicate to non-believers that church introductory courses to Christianity and the teachings of Jesus are still relevant, the majority of people in our country do not sign up for Alpha courses or attend guest services in their local church. Admittedly, the church is often presented incorrectly in TV soaps and online commentaries, which does not help the situation at all.

According to a Tearfund European Social Study published in 2002, the UK stood as the fourth lowest country for church attendance in Europe, marginally ahead of Hungary and France. Worryingly, forecasters predicted a further decline of 55% between the years of 1980 to 2020. This is the reality, and it is not easy on the eyes. But this is not just our reality, it is one we have to pass on to the upcoming generation who will face a harder task to grow and evolve the Evangelical church in the UK.

Considering the spiritual state of play however, let us ask this question: Does the reality change the truth? Or let us look at it this way; has the character of God altered during the decline of the UK church?

We have already explored the rapid changes of spiritual perspective during the Pray4Muamba campaign. But coupled with the potential for spiritual adaptation, we must also look at the resolute reliability of God. In John Ortberg's well-written book *God is Closer Than we Think*, he writes: 'He is never farther than a prayer away. All it takes is the barest effort, the lift of a finger. Every moment – this moment right now, as you read these words – is the "one timeless moment" of divine endowment, of life with God.'

Ortberg goes on to argue: 'The central promise in the Bible is not, "I will forgive you," although of course that promise is there. It is not the promise of life after death, although we are offered that as well. The most frequent promise in the Bible is, "I will be with you." '

Even though hundreds of thousands responded to the Muamba family prayer request, it is still hard to imagine an environment of prayerful sensitivity when the state of our own churches seems more desperate than ever. But we must not cloud the incredible truth of God with the challenging statistics of reality. The statistics should merely spur us on to rethink the shapes, styles and entry points for those new to the Christian message, but they should not take our eyes off the truth; God has not changed.

One of the suggestions I have been posing to my Christian brothers and sisters here in York, is to consider moving the starting line in conversations from introductory Christian course, to talking directly about Jesus. That is not to say we should not be giving a full and honest account of how *we* came to believe in Christ, but in terms of an invitation to faith, why not encourage people to do exactly what Jesus spoke about on the mount? Have we considered encouraging our friends and family members who would not call themselves Christians to close their doors, turn their phones on silent and pray to God in Jesus' name for, or about, the happenings in their lives? Do we have faith enough to allow God to answer the prayers of creation in the hope that they may begin to rely more on God and less on themselves?

I will always remember a conversation I had with Luke Smith, church relations manager for fusion ministries and core team leader of G2 Church in York. We were involved in an evangelistic football project back in 2007 and subsequently saw one of the football players begin to attend our church. As soon as our friend and teammate Tony walked into the service, I was delighted. I knew how rare it was to see one of the lads take an interest in the things of Jesus, and afterwards I spoke with Luke with much excitement. Luke, however, displayed a more muted reaction. He said: 'It's great that we've seen a new face in church today, but that's not what it's all about. I'll be more excited when I'm standing in front of Jesus on the last day and Tony is standing beside me. My ambition isn't to see more people attending church, but to see more people develop a Christian faith. I want to see Tony look to Jesus.'

The conversation challenged me because until then I had always envisaged faith as something developed as a result of visiting church services or an introductory course a few times. But the truth is that those starting lines are just some of the ways people can experience first faith and not all. We can see from scripture that the ways people start their journeys with God are many and varied. Saul was levelled by the voice of Jesus during a walk, the first disciples met Christ in their place of work and Moses was taken back by a bush on fire!

So if the first steps of faith can take place during a shift at work or on a walk, what part does prayer play? Is prayer itself a fitting starting line for those looking to encounter God? And if it is, why do I so often feel it is more productive to hand a flimsy piece of paper with details of a church service to a friend than encourage them to start communing with their saviour themselves? Is my hope that someone attends a church service or that they discover the love and truth of Christ? That is not to say that both cannot go hand in hand of course; in fact, I would argue that God's ideal for those who believe is to be part of a community of Christians who meet regularly. But surely my priority for those searching for truth should be to proclaim how accessible God is now since Jesus' paid the ultimate price for humanity's rebellion. If the curtain of religiosity was well and truly torn at the moment of crucifixion, allowing everyone access to God through faith in Christ, surely how someone begins in the faith is not the paramount issue. The issue also cannot be numbers attending a church service or an introductory Christian course, but the numbers of those praying to God and developing their knowledge of the one we call Jesus.

Oswald Chambers, prominent early twentieth-century minister and teacher, was committed to seeing individuals dedicating time to devotion, prayer and Bible reading. During his incredible ministry, he argued that communicating with God was more important than anything else. He once said: 'Prayer does not fit us for the greater work; prayer is the greater work.'

And as we look to see more of those around us engage with the message of Jesus, I believe we must push prayer to the forefront of the journey for truth. In twenty years people will be explaining to their children what happened to Fabrice Muamba. Many, many parents will tell their kids how they tweeted, blogged or commented on the Pray4Muamba campaign. They will explain how there was an incredible sense of unity in and around the football world and how medical experts were baffled by one young man's recovery. Questions about prayer will be asked. And whatever side of the theism fence we sit on, the evidence suggests that prayer can often be the benchmark for change. Sometimes the change can be seen in an external situation, but more often than not, the change occurs internally.

Like many who have come to faith from a non-churched background, I can remember lots of the more 'serious' prayers I have spoken in my life. Some of my prayers saw miraculous responses while others seemed to fly out on a one-way ticket to the almighty. But regardless of the outcomes, I can testify that the very act of praying drew me closer to God. And though we Evangelicals know this to be true, it is incredibly easy to let this truth fall down the pecking order when something shiny arrives in Christendom. The truth is that there is nothing shiny, cute or polished about the sorts of prayers we are told to pray in the Bible. It is not easy to close the world out and begin to bare one's soul to an invisible God.

Coupled with the lack of va-va-voom surrounding prayer, reality has its own way of distracting searchers and persuading believers that nobody outside the church would be interested in this archaic, obsolete way of life.

Of course there are those who will deem prayer as obsolete. Some of my closest friends still think I've been won over by a religious cult due to my decision to follow Jesus. But we cannot use the fact that some will refuse to pray as a reason not to encourage others to pray. In Paul's second letter to the church in Corinth, he uses a wonderful turn of phrase to illustrate this point:

> For we are to God the pleasing aroma of Christ among those who are being saved and those who are perishing. To the one we are an aroma that brings death; to the other, an aroma that brings life. And who is equal to such a task? Unlike so many, we do not peddle the word of God for profit. On the contrary, in Christ we speak before God with sincerity, as those sent from God.
>
> 2 Corinthians 2:15–17

Paul knows there are those who respond to the message of Jesus negatively, but he reminds us that there are those who are on the brink of tasting the life-affirming qualities only God can bring.

So as we are reminded that many people would be, right now, willing to take their first steps of faith through sincere prayer, we too must pray that our soul is sensitive to those genuinely searching for their creator. As senior pastor and author Bill Hybels puts it: 'Authentic Christianity is a supernatural walk with a living, dynamic, communicating God.' (*Too Busy Not To Pray*)

There are supernatural walks that have not yet started in the lives of those around us. There are empty prayer canvasses in the lives of our friends who are waiting to be told their souls can speak at anytime. If only people knew they already had the tools to get off the starting line. The truth is many do not yet know they are on the starting line at all.

## UNKNOWN TO KNOWN

One of the priorities for the New Testament leaders was to make an 'unknown' God known among the Gentiles. There had never been a general assumption that the Gentiles would come to faith until Jesus addressed them as people who could have their own faith journey. It was offensive to many religious folk that Christ was not just calling the Gentiles 'blessed' but he went one further and called them friends. I would argue that the same assumption that existed amongst the religious folk back then still exists today. The secular world seems a million miles away from the Sunday service. Their worship is arguably kept for materialism, academia and physical gratification. And sure there is truth in this, but we should draw instant parallels between the *now* and the *then*.

The Apostle Paul took a massive step of faith in the Book of Acts and addressed some of the most freethinking minds in his region. One of his impressive short talks changed some of his listeners' lives forever. His reputation for speaking about God in a totally accessible way spread around Athens and he was called to speak publicly. This is what was said:

> Paul then stood up in the meeting of the Areopagus and said: 'People of Athens! I see that in every way you are very religious. For as I walked around and looked carefully at your objects of worship, I even found an altar with this inscription: to an unknown god. So you are ignorant of the very thing you worship—and this is what I am going to proclaim to you.

> The God who made the world and everything in it is the Lord of heaven and earth and does not live in temples built by human hands. And he is not served by human hands, as if he needed anything. Rather, he himself gives everyone life and breath and everything else. From one man he made all the nations, that they should inhabit the whole earth; and he marked out their appointed times in history and the boundaries of their lands. God did this so that they would seek him and perhaps reach out for him and find him, though he is not far from any one of us. For in him we live and move and have our being. As some of your own poets have said, "We are his offspring."

Therefore since we are God's offspring, we should not think that the divine being is like gold or silver or stone – an image made by human design and skill. In the past God overlooked such ignorance, but now he commands all people everywhere to repent. For he has set a day when he will judge the world with justice by the man he has appointed. He has given proof of this to everyone by raising him from the dead.'

Acts 17:22–31

Paul knew the Athenians were misguided in terms of their understanding of prayer and worship. But this did not lead Paul to think the Athenian culture was lost. He saw their 'unknown' deity and pointed directly to Christ as a 'known' deity. The passage goes on to explain that some of the crowd began their own journeys of faith right there and then. For Paul, the starting line of faith began with Jesus. It was not about attaining an academic understanding of Jesus, or an emotional experience of Jesus, or even a physical manifestation of Jesus. Paul argued true faith was built on approaching Jesus with awe and reverence. And this is what I am praying for those around me. My hope is that they would not just feel at home in church, but that they would find a new sense of 'home' in Christ.

Not for a second would I propose to replace intro-ductory Christian courses with solitary prayer. There is great value in learning and discussing the things of Christ in a group scenario. But I would argue that if Jesus could encounter humankind so wonderfully in his ministry, on both an individual level and a corporate level, is it possible to consider a culture where we encourage similar encounters among the secular world?

I long to see a mindset adopted amongst Christians in the UK that inspires sincere, honest and long-lasting prayer within secular circles. I pray not for a replacement starting line for those outside of the faith, but an alternative one. In my own life I am testing this idea out. I am sharing Jesus' teachings on the simplicity of prayer with my friends who do not think they have the tools to pray. My hope is that the mumbled, fragmented chats between man and God will become the first steps of faith for thousands. And that those men and women of faith would go on to prioritise prayer in their families, churches and places of work.

## GREEN LIGHT THEOLOGY

> *Without continual growth and progress, such words as improvement, achievement, and success have no meaning.*
>
> Benjamin Franklin

There are certain environments or 'seasons' when it's easier and more appropriate to talk to others about the things of Jesus. Some people find the periods around Christmas or Easter an inspiration to answer the big questions posed by close friends and family members. Other believers are often involved in theological debates during a church wedding, or during the aftermath of a funeral. It is true that when we share the truths behind prayer with those in secular circles, we must be sensitive to the season and circumstance. After all, Jesus himself showed incredible sympathy with those he came to save, including us.

But one misconception that often sneaks in through the back door of a church or house group is that only certain types of Christians can talk to others about the faith. A congregation will pick out the best communicator or the most coherent at apologetics and take solace in the fact that at least someone is taking prayer to those outside of the building.

And though there are clear teachings in the New Testament regarding those more gifted in communicating the message of Jesus, it is important to remember two sacred truths:

1.  We live in an age where the Holy Spirit is eager to support *any* believer sharing their faith.
2.  Not even Billy Graham has managed to save one soul, but has merely pointed to the one who can.

Many of my friends at church often express their frustration at not feeling able to talk about the power of prayer with those around them. They feel unequipped to bring up such a discussion and the idea of them asking one of their non-believing friends if they'd like to pray is utterly terrifying. I often pose the question, 'What would need to change for you to be more confident in sharing the message with others?' The responses I get from my Christian friends are often very similar. They talk about not losing their relationships, not feeling like an idiot and not wasting their time. And as I chat more about their reservations in talking about prayer, I soon find that their perspective on how the Holy Spirit responds to a watered mustard seed of faith in secularism, is warped. Where many Christians believe we live in an age when the things of Jesus have been given a red light and ordered to stop, the truth is we live in an age where Jesus himself has given us the green light and told us to go. (Matthew 28:19)

Imagine for a second that there were people in your life who were just inches away from beginning their own personal prayer life with the same God who you have been communicating with all this time. Imagine if the person who you assumed was frosty towards the Gospel was indeed the one who will go on to plant the most compassionate and dynamic church in the UK. Imagine if that friend who has always seemed to have the worst luck in the world sees a prayer unequivocally answered. It's hard to imagine these things in the hustle and bustle of secularism, but we only have to look at the heroes of the New Testament to see that God is indeed capable of using prayer to change those sorts of lives.

A few years ago a Bible teacher in Birmingham asked me this: 'What has changed spiritually since Peter preached and saw 5000 converts?' I pondered the question for a while and after looking at the fundamentals regarding post-resurrection, post-Pentecost, and full-Gospel times, I had to answer him with, 'Nothing has changed'. And indeed it has not. We live in an age where people are starting their prayer journeys all over the world every single day. Churches are growing rapidly in countries where the Christian message is prohibited. The lights for seeing non-believers become prayerful are green. We live in green-light times, if only we would believe.

I will never lose a sense of wonder and delight at how the world was united in prayer for Fabrice Muamba. It was a story that grabbed at every atom in my soul. But the truth is that we do not need an internationally broadcast event to see people take steps forward in prayer. God did not suddenly become more visible or indeed more powerful when Muamba stunned the medical world with his recovery.

If faith was an issue of global finance, the stocks and shares for prayer would have been open for thousands of years, and yet we treat inclusive prayer like a bankrupt entity, frozen on Wall Street. We forget that prayer has shaped lives, communities and nations throughout history. The prophets who collated much of the Old Testament frequently called their whole country to pray, before anything else.

Christian teacher Oswald Chambers, who ministered powerfully at the turn of the twentieth century, strived to live under the green light of spiritual potential. He once wrote:

> If you obey God in the first thing He shows you, then He instantly opens up the next truth to you. You could read volumes on the work of the Holy Spirit, when five minutes of total, uncompromising obedience would make things as clear as sunlight. Don't say, 'I suppose I will understand these things someday!' You can understand them now. And it is not study that brings understanding to you, but obedience. Even the smallest bit of obedience opens heaven, and the deepest truths of God immediately become yours. Yet God will never reveal more truth about Himself to you, until you have obeyed what you know already.'

And when all is said and done, if we have been given grace enough to pray to God, we have been commanded to share this grace with others. One of the greatest responses I have had from a non-believer was when I emailed him with this simple sentence: 'Hi mate, hope all is well. Just a quick email, you know I pray, yeah? Well this morning I will be praying for three specific friends and you're one of them. Is there anything worrying you at present? Let me know mate, Alexander.'

My friend's response was 1500 words long where he poured his heart out to me. He is now taking his own steps of prayer and currently working his way through the Gospels. However, if you had seen how nervous I was before sending that email, you would have probably recommended I had a lie down. My laptop screen felt like a blaring lamp used for torture. Each word dropped onto the computer with a heavy thud; my pride begging me to reconsider.

Whatever the scenario, it will always feel unnatural to encourage those outside the church to step forward into prayer, because Evangelicals are in the minority. And when faced with a secular majority in our personal lives, the task of presenting an aged faith is daunting. But let us consider this: what if the Muamba family had not passed that message onto the press? What if they had used a different word, a more modern word, a culturally acceptable word? I have come to the conclusion on more than one occasion that sometimes we have to embrace the awkwardness involved with contemporary evangelism and stand tall.

Things are changing in the UK for the church. I believe that the age of stadium events for altar calls has passed in the West. TV evangelists are becoming cannon fodder for stand-up comics, who mimic their attempts to coerce viewers to hand over credit card details. The next generation can spot a manipulation attempt at twenty paces, rendering many forms of old-school communication obsolete. I would argue that now is the time for honesty, vulnerability and authenticity. My hope is to see twenty-first-century believers cut through the monstrosity of philosophical pride and offer their hands and feet to those living without prayer. Too many of us have opted to dig our heels in the ground as a response to stones thrown by the voices of atheism, as if the creator of all things may cease to exist if we lose a debate. As I search the Scriptures and meditate on the person of Jesus, I honestly believe it's not about *debating*, it is about *relating*. And from the examples of answered prayer we see in Scripture, we can confidently say that God is willing and ready to help us relate to every single human we encounter if we too would pray for help.

To live a life that is scattered with opportunities to invite others to pray, calls for the discipline of denying oneself daily. It is a journey lit not by fancy lights and famous names, but one where real people, real pain and real lives are engaged. And the sobering thought is this; it is a lifestyle we can adopt right now. We all have names in our phonebooks and email accounts who may need to be told the access to God is now open through prayer in Jesus' name. We all have loved ones who are standing over the canyon of faith awaiting further instruction. And so, even as I write this, I too am thinking about who I can be engaging with through prayer. My close friend recovering from a torn cruciate ligament, my neighbour battling with alcoholism, my old house-mate who is currently in mourning? I too am trying to stamp this question onto the frontal lobe of my soul: 'Who can I lead closer to prayerfulness today?'

Nine years ago I was studying for my degree, and during one of the modules called 'engaging with an unknown audience', the lecturer encouraged us to walk into the streets of Scarborough and York pre-senting an alternative message to the onlookers. It was a bizarre and vague brief for a group of 19 year olds. Some of my fellow students waltzed through the high street like bad ballroom dancers. Others staged a romantic picnic in the middle of the busy square. I thought long and hard about my 'alterna-tive message' and chose to stand solitude in the city centre with a large piece of card which read:

## WOULD ANYONE LIKE TO PRAY?

My lecturers were eager to see the results but I was becoming more and more nervous as shoppers began to stop and stare directly at me. My fear soon subsided when after just a few seconds, a man in a suit approached me. He put his arm on my shoulder and said: 'Mate, I don't know who you are, but I've just left my mum in hospital and I asked God for a sign as I left. That was ten minutes ago. And here you are standing with a sign that reads would anyone like to pray? So, yes, I would please.'

I prayed with Geoff for a few minutes as onlookers stood in amazement. For hours I was approached with prayer requests. I prayed with people worried about family members serving in the army overseas. I prayed with students missing home and heartbroken folk coping with break-ups. One man prayed he'd be able to survive the passing of Frankie, his beloved cat.

It was during this project I began to see how many people are still open to praying about real issues in their lives. As I stood in the north east with a huge prayerful invitation to those around me, I felt the scepticism sitting in my heart being eroded away. Those who came forward to request prayer were real people, with real lives. Men in suits, women with children, teachers, builders, lapsed Catholics and Buddhists. They all came forward. And I believe the reason they came forward was because there is something of God that draws from the human soul when prayer is on offer.

I knew I had to adopt a new perspective. Prayer is a powerful starting line for those looking to find out more about why they are on this planet. And as we engage with others, we should remember that nothing is too small to pray about; every prayer matters to the Father. Whether it's the heartfelt cries of a miracle regarding an injured footballer called Fabrice, or living life without a pet cat called Frankie, God loves prayer.

Looking back on my personal story of how I came to faith, there is no doubt that prayer played an incredible part. I was not exactly the ideal candidate for the popular conceptions of Christianity. In truth,

I bullied the first Christian I ever met. But thanks to that particular believer's perseverance, I can now testify to eleven years of knowing the one who is called Jesus. There was not a month that went by that this Christian did not ask me if I wanted to pray. Sometimes she would ask if there was anything she could pray for me. Five years after first meeting this uncompromising girl of faith, I knelt in a church foyer in Cardiff and acknowledged Jesus as 'Lord' for the first time. I am walking proof that the average guy can still find a genuine faith amid a seemingly secular society. I have now had the incredible privilege of sharing the truth about prayer with others. And some of the most significant moments in my life have been seeing friends turn to Jesus in prayer. I hope you too will begin to see these moments more in your lives.

What is the Pray4 Principle? In essence, it's a prayerful unity within secular society. It is a reminder that we live in an age receptive to prayer. It is an encouragement that, despite the colossal force of media outlets which surround us, nothing will ever delete prayer from this world. It is a sign that says whatever humans create, whether it be buildings made of stone or communicative software tools like Twitter, the Holy Spirit can blow in and around the details. Prayers can line the walls of a home, pub or church. They can take centre stage on an online phenomena and make national news. The Pray4 Principle shows us that prayer is as important today as it always has been. Prayer can be the last word, the first word, the final destination and the starting line. It has the power to unite cultures separated by oceans and traditions. Prayer does not require academia, experience or even much faith. It does not belong anywhere specific but everywhere specific. Praying is a breathing mechanism for the human soul. It overrides the human condition and anchors the individual to an immovable deity. And it is not going anywhere. The Bible teaches us that in these end days the believers will talk to the King, as they will throughout eternity.

## FROM HERE

It is almost one year since the Pray4Muamba campaign took flight. I have found that, despite revisiting the events, studying the news reports and medical summaries, I am mostly drawn to the public's reaction. I have found, like any 'spiritual' event, it is always worth writing the big questions down in hindsight to help process the issue.

One of the first questions to ask is probably the most obvious. How do we personally view the whole prayer campaign?

Do we view it simply as a sympathy fad for a desperate man? Or do we see the potential for spiritual awakening in an age where prayer is still important? Was the campaign a sign of the fickle nature of the modern human or a signpost to something bigger?

## SCEPTICISM

In the planning stages of starting this writing project, an atheist friend of mine asked me outright if I believe God healed Fabrice Muamba. It is a question that leads to a thousand more questions surrounding healings, God's will and divine intervention.

My answer was simply that I believed for reasons unknown, a series of seemingly impossible events took place that led to what can only be described as a miracle. When you have specialist cardiologists referring to a recovery as miraculous, one has to allow for the possibility that there is more going on than what meets the eye. We have to make allowances for the possibility that what we see, hear, touch, taste and smell is not the endgame. I admitted that I have no idea *why* Muamba survived the ordeal, and why many others have never recovered from similar events. I also admitted that it's impossible to *prove* that it was definitely divine intervention that took place during the Spurs versus Bolton match. However, that does not mean we can flippantly write off the possibility that something beyond our understanding was taking place in the body of Fabrice Muamba and the souls of the watching world.

I have to admit that, like my friend, I do still have the tendency to harbour scepticism when hearing of miraculous healings. If I had been out of the country for the whole Pray4Muamba campaign, I too would have struggled with the idea that God was leading the proceedings. You see, scepticism is part and parcel of the human experience. Some believers attribute every bizarre event to the work of God, as they battle the internal doubts plaguing their spiritual journey. Many others believe the complete opposite and claim that nothing is of God, to reduce the risk of being proved wrong or coming across as a weirdo. So where can the healthy approach be found?

In Paul's first letter to the Thessalonian Church, he addressed the issue of how we should approach spiritual issues with hindsight. Speaking specifically about the notion of prophecy, Paul highlighted and modelled a mature way to processing the miraculous:

> Do not quench the Spirit. Do not treat prophecies with contempt but test them all; hold on to what is good, reject every kind of evil.
>
> 1 Thessalonians 5:1922

We must not shy away from the idea that there is an unseen Holy Spirit operating in the physical world. But simultaneously, we should be mature enough to test the seemingly unnatural circumstances so that nobody becomes mislead or confused. I meet a lot of people who sit firmly in one of two camps. The phrase, 'That's God,' seems to run off the tip of many people's tongues with an air of over-familiarity increasing my natural instinct to become sceptical. In the other camp, many people cling only to the facts at hand, even if those facts point to the work of a higher force. It is a war between the sceptic and the assumer. One refuses to attribute anything to God, the other attributes everything. Paul argues none of them are healthy.

So how then do we 'test' this realm of the strange and bizarre? I would emphasise that our first question should be if the circumstances fit or contradict the teachings set out for us in Scripture. Looking back at Muamba's recovery, we can see correlations between examples of answered prayer in the Gospel accounts, and the story surrounding Fabrice. When Jesus met with those with a physical need, he met individuals facing situations out of their control. Whether it be a blind man desperate for vision or the lifeless Lazarus, the starting point often seemed to be with a powerless individual.

Physical ailments befell men and women from different backgrounds throughout Jesus' ministry, regardless of the beliefs they upheld. It is important to see that often there is no clear reason behind illness, physical ailments or injuries. And if we cannot sit comfortably with the idea that some things just happen, then we leave ourselves open to empty superstition. If we are constantly assigning spiritual reasons for physical challenges we no longer believe in a God who operates on a different level to us, but a God who can be boxed up and explained in his entirety.

Throughout the whole Book of Job we see that God never explains to the main character *why* he is allowing him to suffer. And as humans, like Job, we need to be ok with not knowing. After all, even Job was humble enough to admit this towards the end of the account:

> You asked, 'Who is this that obscures my plans without knowledge?' Surely I spoke of things I did not understand, things too wonderful for me to know.
>
> Job 42:3

Continuing to think of how we can righteously test the seemingly supernatural, as Paul highlights to the Thessalonians, we need to hold on to what is good. This may sound like a strange thing to do under extreme circumstances, but I would argue that *goodness* is often a symptom of God's presence in a situation. The Book of James sums this up poetically:

> Every good and perfect gift is from above, coming down from the Father of the heavenly lights, who does not change like shifting shadows.
>
> James 1:17

However, we must not confuse what we see or feel as goodness with God's tangible goodness. During the Pray4Muamba campaign I saw something of God's character in the entire process not just the miraculous recovery. As people prayed, communed, hoped, mourned and loved, I saw genuine goodness. In the Bible, from the first tribes right up to the crucifixion, we see a God who specialises in bringing goodness to the surface of a painful situation. One of the tests for what is, or is not, a divine intervention has to be whether or not goodness is a genuine fruit. Jesus picked up on this notion after teaching on prayer:

> Which of you fathers, if your son asks for a fish, will give him a snake instead? Or if he asks for an egg, will give him a scorpion? If you then, though you are evil, know how to give good gifts to your children, how much more will your Father in heaven give the Holy Spirit to those who ask him!
>
> Luke 11:11–13

When we see goodness coming out of a bad situation, we should be prepared to accept that God may be at work. The Pray4Muamba campaign was drenched in goodness, despite it being founded on what was a tragic occurrence. For me, this strongly suggests that God had an agenda somewhere in the process.

I would argue the third test would be if the event itself resulted in people thinking more about God or those involved. In our culture of sporting idols, TV celebrities and media egos, we are surrounded by the worship of humanity. Unfortunately this creeps into Christendom also. Across the Western world we see examples of Christian brands boasting more and more about their achievements, vision and hard work, moving the raw message of Jesus further away from the limelight. Religious figures carry a reputation of a strong gifting or an amazing ministry, posing the question; 'Who is the main character here, the leader or the saviour?'

The reason I strongly believe that God was at work throughout the Pray4Muamba campaign isn't primarily that Fabrice defeated all the odds and made a full recovery, but that at the end of it, he pointed directly at Jesus. This attitude of worship is the clincher for me. When those directly involved in the miracle talk more about Jesus than they do of themselves, I can safely assume that God has been getting their hands dirty in a situation. For we know that God is not interested in raising up human idols to be followed by the masses. In the life of Christ we see the greatest being of all giving praise to the Father. The ultimate test of whether or not something is good is if it's from God. And Scripture tells us time and time again that God's ultimate will for humanity is to get to know *him* better. Fabrice Muamba has testified live in front of the press that the campaign was not about him, but about God. Every miracle has to give the last words to the one who gives and takes life.

## HOW NOW?

I have found myself drawn to praying more since researching the Pray4Muamba campaign. The goodness that pointed to the work of God's hand has changed my sceptical perspective on what God can and cannot do in twenty-first century secular England. My prayers have become less like a wish list since starting this project, but I have become more confident in revealing my desires and struggles to God who longs for real friendship with creation.

My prayer for you is the same as it is for me. I pray that you become more honest, vulnerable and authentic in your own prayer life, as well as in your invitations to those around you. That your spiritual sphere becomes ever-growing and inclusive for strangers and friends to soak their weary lives.

I pray that those around you do not just describe you as a person with a 'good heart' but as someone with God on their lips. And not a religious God either. I long to see secular thinkers refer to our God as one who is full of emotion, dynamism, love and laughter.

I hope that those who have identified themselves as believers in this age learn to communicate the peace, compassion and adventure that is Jesus. And that we would be remembered as followers of Christ who invited others to pray, regardless of their backgrounds or beliefs, accents or appearance. I pray the UK church is seen as a great cheerleader for the goodness that God continues to bring to the lives of those looking for meaning.

And I long to see Christians in the driving seat of such movements as Pray4Muamba. Would we be those who pioneer the next prayer campaign or sit on the sidelines and throw stones of scepticism? Would we take the beautiful notions of the Pray4 Principle and walk side by side with those new to prayer, or sit comfortably in our evangelical, academic understanding of God? Is it possible to see our communities hold prayer as close to their hearts as they do their local football team? From witnessing how the world reacted to Muamba's plight, I believe it is.

But ultimately I pray we show people Jesus. That our egos and agendas would be dumped at the foot of the cross and we would long to see our lost world find their identity in the Prince of Peace and not in hollow religion or angry beliefs.

It is fitting then to close this exploration with the model prayer taught to us by Jesus. It is a prayer that unites all believers and one I am happy to pray with you now:

> One day Jesus was praying in a certain place. When he finished, one of his disciples said to him, 'Lord, teach us to pray, just as John taught his disciples.'
>
> He said to them, 'When you pray, say:
>
> Father, hallowed be your name, your kingdom come.
>
> Give us each day our daily bread.
>
> Forgive us our sins, for we also forgive everyone who sins against us.

And lead us not into temptation.'

Then Jesus said to them, 'Suppose you have a friend, and you go to him at midnight and say, "Friend, lend me three loaves of bread; a friend of mine on a journey has come to me, and I have no food to offer him." And suppose the one inside answers, "Don't bother me. The door is already locked, and my children and I are in bed. I can't get up and give you anything." I tell you, even though he will not get up and give you the bread because of friendship, yet because of your shameless audacity he will surely get up and give you as much as you need.

So I say to you: Ask and it will be given to you; seek and you will find; knock and the door will be opened to you. For everyone who asks receives; the one who seeks finds; and to the one who knocks, the door will be opened.'

Luke 11:1–10

Amen.

It has been an honour to tackle such an important and timely issue as prayer in secular society. I know there are countless experiences of answered prayer up and down the homes of the British Isles. I would love to hear about your relationship with prayer, whether you have been practicing it for decades, or praying for the first time. Above everything, we must remember that God is love and nothing we can do can earn his grace. We must remember that Jesus gave his life freely, allowing us to live our lives prayerfully without cost. Nobody has the monopoly on how we should pray. All of us have been created uniquely because God intended it that way. God wants us to be ourselves in prayer, honest, vulnerable and personal. Let us not become carbon copies of our religious ancestors, but look to spark a new-found interest and fascination with how we communicate with God, through God's son Jesus. That is my prayer for this brilliant country, which I am thankful to God for putting me in.

Please let me know your experiences with prayer via Twitter, I'd love to hear from you. @randomalexander

# Afterword

## A PRAYER THAT CHANGED A LIFE: THE AUTHOR'S STORY

During this project I have often referred to 'my story' in an attempt to personalise how I have come to understand the Pray4 Principle. Here follows an abridged account of how a lad who was a professed atheist at the age of six became a believer a decade later.

***

The message of Jesus had eluded me growing up in a town described by journalists as 'East Germany without the tanks'. Year by year, my birthplace featured on Channel Four's Top Ten Worst British Towns with life expectancy lower than war-ravaged Iraq, and the average age to start smoking at just nine years old. Questions of faith were not realistic. The reality was that there was more chance of finding an alcohol-fuelled brawl in the high street than finding a job.

Subsequently, the message of Jesus was tucked away in advent calendars and Christmas trinkets, largely purchased by the older generations who never blasphemed. I was born and raised in Merthyr Tydfil, South Wales, and for that I am truly thankful.

My mother was a single parent supporting three boys, of which I was the middle in age. With the help of two immense grandparents, Mr and Mrs Williams, our family had some great times in Merthyr. My inaugural experience of the notion of faith came as I watched Cameroon in the 1990 World Cup. Cameroon reached the semi-finals that year and during their matches a number of their players would often make the sign of the cross, perplexing my childlike brain. I queried this bizarre ritual with my mother, who told me it was their way of expressing their faith in Jesus. I then asked my mum if Jesus was God. She told me she did not believe there was a God. And that was that. I had heard enough to make up my mind. As a callow, six-year-old atheist, I was quite content.

At the age of 11, I attended a comprehensive school in an eerie old castle called Cyfarthfa (in English it means the 'fox's lair'). All the lads from various primary schools eyed up their fresh adversaries as we were flung together in form groups. On hearing the names of strangers being called out in the gymnasium, I saw a girl sitting opposite me, smiling. The unusual thing was that she appeared to be the only one expressing joy in the whole building. I turned to my new best friend Jamie and asked him if he knew who this human glow-worm was. He replied, 'Her name is Lois, she is weird, she talks to Jesus'.

For the next five years I got to know this 'weird' girl who indeed thought she could speak to Jesus. The more I got to know her, the more I was exposed to her Christian faith and unique approach to living as a teenage girl in Merthyr Tydfil. Whilst most of my female companions were out drinking by the age of 13, and making sure they were not left behind on the 'virgin bus', Lois talked about how God's plan for our lives was to live in freedom.

To be honest, though I was drawn to her uncompromising stance on the existence of a creator and the need for a saviour, I became livid that she was more interested in Jesus than pandering to my quest for attention. She refused to leave me to the dogs of valley culture, which saw some of my friends addicted to illegal substances before they were old enough to drive. It was not as if she was perfect, she just believed there was a perfect plan for anyone who would look towards Jesus. Somehow it annoyed me.

At 16 I had formed a habit in my life of bullying this teenage evangelist. While she refused to kick with the fray and drink cider out of plastic bottles, I was busy playing a decent standard of Saturday football and enjoying Merthyr's binge-drinking culture. Despite her efforts to tell me about Jesus, I was dead set on becoming either a footballer, an actor or a Royal Marine. None of the aforementioned aspirations involved Jesus.

In the summer of 2000, I experienced what most of the lads had gone through already: my first proper beating. Three blokes from a different part of the valley took the liberty of dragging me from a pub doorway, through a forest and onto a viaduct overlooking the town, before they kicked me unconscious. As I endured the event, which left my head split open, my face slightly altered and my rib cage damaged, I remember thinking about the existence of God. One of the lads involved told me he was going to throw me off the viaduct. At that point I wondered how sad it would be if I died and Lois was actually right. What if Jesus was who he claimed to be and I had spent the last five years bullying one of his followers? The pain of the kick-in did not really hit me until I sobered up the next day. Suffice to say I became friends with ibuprofen in the ensuing weeks.

As the year 2000 tagged in 2001, my mate Gibbon and I decided to get a train as far north as we could afford to and celebrate New Year's Eve. We ended up in the quaint surroundings of Barnard Castle, County Durham. Our false IDs worked a charm in the hotel bar where we shared a cheeky cigarette, laughing at the strange variations on the English accent. While we reminisced about the year that had passed, we found it fitting to make New Year's resolutions.

Gibbon took a contrary approach to the whole idea as he vowed to drink more, eat more and increase other activities in his life, some of which do not bear mention in this publication. Competitive as ever, I wanted to raise the bar. Scanning the room for inspiration I clocked a huge lounge window covered in a crystal pattern of frost. Beyond it was the towering spire of a church rising from the multitude of snowy roofs in the town centre. It then occurred to me that for all my confident opinions about the existence of God (or lack thereof), I had never experienced a church service myself. I turned to Gibbon and said I would go to church once in the New Year. He almost swallowed his cigarette. He warned me that I may not be allowed into a church given my fascination with alcohol and my love of football.

The weeks following my Barnard Castle visit were very strange. One of the rugby lads took a disliking to me for something I had said to him in school and challenged me to a fight at 3.10pm in the foyer one Friday afternoon. I had been involved in quite a few fights up to this point in my life, but something inside me had changed. I had no idea what, but it was like the cogs of my DNA were slowing down in preparation for something new.

The fight came and went. During Monday's lunch break, I sat on Lois's table with a million questions about the human soul, the existence of a creator and the need for a saviour. However, being a typical teenage lad, I carried far too much arrogance to ask about those sorts of things. Nevertheless, the following Sunday morning I woke up, threw on a pair of jeans, watched some football highlights and walked to church. It was terrifying.

I sat at the back and chewed on the dust in the air wondering which cheap so-and-so designed wooden benches for people to sit on. In front of me, along a shelf running the length of the pew in front, a hymn book sat proudly alongside a Bible. (Both of which I knew nothing about). Then a strange man got to his feet, strode to the lectern and spoke for too long about things he knew too much about. As my attention waned I sensed the eyes of the congregation on me, it felt like an episode from *The Wicker Man*. I honestly thought I might be sacrificed at the end of the service.

Lois and I laughed about my first experience of church and I was later invited to a youth music event in Cardiff on a weekend. I accepted the invitation and before I knew it I was surrounded by hundreds of teenagers crying and jumping to songs about Jesus. Feeling self-conscious I eased out of the All Nation's Centre, hoping nobody would notice I had been the guy who never raised his hands or jumped up and down.

As I sat next to a gigantic vending machine, I was joined by Pete, one of Lois's friends. He was a few years older than me but made nothing of it.

On hearing my story of faithlessness, Pete shared something with me I had never heard. Apparently Jesus said he could offer life to the max not just for the disciples but for every human who walked the planet after his death and resurrection. It made sense to me that a claim as big as that needed to be considered at least once in my life.

So on 16 February 2001, I bowed my head next to a drinks machine in Cardiff and said, 'Lord Jesus,' quietly. It was the first time I had acknowledged Jesus in the way he asked us to in the Bible. I did not fall on the floor. I did not grow a pair of fangs. I did not levitate. I just knew in my head and in my heart that Jesus was the 'Lord' and as tangible as the can of cola I was holding. It was a case of accepting the fact that I was not the centre of my own life any more. Until that moment I had been wearing the captain's armband every day. But in the quietness of a secluded foyer, I openly confessed that Jesus was Lord; I believed in my heart God raised him from the dead although I knew very little of Jesus, except the fact that he was the captain.

From that moment on, I found myself noticing things I had never paid any attention to: stars in the sky, smiles on human faces and the folly of my dogs. I was more grateful for the game of football, I started reading school books with an unprecedented passion and my love for Jesus started to take shape.

I revisited my local church to help out as opposed to walk out. I saw my friends as God-breathed human beings and sought to share the message of Jesus with them.

I will be honest, I could not fathom *why* Jesus would model a perfect life, explain the truth about everything and die on a cross for someone as average as me … all to help me become the man God had designed me to be. It did not seem like a fair bargain.

Jesus received a half-hearted, moaning, prideful Welsh teenager as a follower and I received life to the max.

Looking back at the change of events, I understood why the Bible used the term 'born again'. I understood it because I experienced it. Life became *full* as oppose to *busy*. And 11 years on I am still in awe of Jesus, more so now than ever before.

It took a young girl five years of enduring an arrogant, bullish clown, for me to learn the most important lesson of my life. I learnt that *anyone* could have a friendship with God through prayer. In my head I had always assumed Christians were people who had been brought up in a particular religious way. I did not think there was a back door to Christianity for guys like me. I had been wrong. Jesus had left an escape route for those trapped in an incomplete existence. He had written average atheists like me into his blueprints.

It is safe to say I have often looked at the culture of Christendom and felt like a square peg in a round hole. People who have been raised in a church environment often use the phrase 'rough diamond' to sum up my attempt at holiness.

But my encouragement to those who do not feel like they could ever fit into the mould of the typical Christian, is that there is a place for you like there was for Paul the Apostle. There is a seat at the table for anyone ready to start a prayer journey with Jesus. And that is why it is still good news.